*The Pocket Encyclopaedia of*
# Modern Roses

*To my father, Charles Walter Gregory*

Tony Gregory

*The Pocket Encyclopaedia of*
*Modern Roses*

**BLANDFORD PRESS**
POOLE · DORSET

First published in the U.K. 1984 by Blandford Press,
Link House, West Street, Poole, Dorset, BH15 1LL.

Copyright © 1984 Blandford Press Ltd.

Distributed in the United States by
Sterling Publishing Co., Inc.,
2 Park Avenue, New York, N.Y. 10016.

**British Library Cataloguing in Publication Data**

Gregory, T. A. C.
  The pocket encyclopaedia of modern roses.
  1. Roses – Dictionaries
  I. Title
  583′.372′0321          SB411

ISBN 0 7137 1261 9

All rights reserved. No part of this book may
be reproduced or transmitted in any form or by
any means, electronic or mechanical, including
photocopying, recording or any information storage
and retrieval system, without permission in
writing from the Publisher.

Typeset by August Filmsetting, Warrington, Cheshire

Printed in Hong Kong by South China Printing Co.

# Contents

Introduction 6

Acknowledgements 7

The History of the Modern Rose 8

The Story of Floribundas 12

Miniature Roses 13

Classification 14

Explanation of Rose Terms 16

Colour Plates 17–112

Notes on Cultivation 115

Pruning 118

Descriptions of Varieties 122

Index 190

*Errata*
Colour plates:
No. 2 is Apricot Silk,
19 Wendy Cussons,
144 Fashion and 145 Tonnerre.

# Introduction

There have been several epochs in the history of the rose: the establishment of the ancient roses, the discovery of China roses, the breeding of hybrid perpetuals, and the introduction of the hybrid tea. Another event of equal magnitude was the development of the modern garden roses, hybrid teas, floribundas, climbers, miniature and shrub roses. The period 1945–80 saw the most energetic production of roses that were carefully developed for 'everyman's' garden.

At the advent of the period almost every bush hybrid tea seemed to have a neck so thin and weak that the blooms drooped down, or so thick and brittle that they broke off at a touch. Every bloom of quality seemed to ball up and rot on the stem at the least hint of wet weather. Almost all varieties seemed subject to black spot, and white powdery mildew that covered a plant from head to toe was tolerated providing the bloom was exceptional. The climbers were huge and flowered only in the spring, or like the ramblers they were full of mildew and rust. Floribundas, or polyanthas as they were then called, were all single or semi-double, and miniatures were promoted by demonstrating their ability to pass through a wedding ring.

Such was the position when the great hybridists Meilland, McGredy, Tantau, Kordes, Poulsen, Swim, Dickson and their contemporaries opened up the golden age of rose growing. 'Peace', 'Queen Elizabeth' and 'Super Star' roses set a new standard and supplied a market eager to try something new. The rose-growing public perhaps played the key role. They were eager to try new roses, profuse in their acclaim of varieties with outstanding qualities and ruthless in their condemnation and discarding of inferior introductions.

Before the Second World War, it had taken decades for a variety to cross the Atlantic or circulate around Europe, but now varieties were transported, tried and tested worldwide a year or so after they had been introduced in their country of origin. It was interesting to see that the President's Trophy winner in the United Kingdom failed miserably in the United States, whereas a seedling with not much promise in Britain could prove a winner in Australia. With so much international co-operation the breeders could immediately respond to the demand for better 'garden roses' as opposed to exhibition varieties, and as soon as a trend was indicated they could quickly acquire the relevant new 'blood' and develop it. Even rose-growers who were not noted breeders stood a good chance of obtaining winners by crossing two promising parents.

Breeders had previously been concerned with giving their nurseries the 'edge' by having for a few years the exclusive rights to a variety by virtue of the fact that they possessed all the original stock. Plant Breeders Rights legislation in 1964 meant that a royalty could be charged on all protected varieties. Breeders could, thereafter, enjoy an income directly related to their efforts and were able to concentrate more time and resources on the hybridising side of their business. Even better roses were the result.

It is important that the outstanding roses of this post-war period should be recorded and documented along with some outstanding varieties which span the break from the previous era. Their part on the world stage was very brief, but proper tribute should be paid to their significance.

## Acknowledgements

I would like to pay tribute to the late Henry Edland, who wrote the first Pocket Encyclopaedia of Roses, and to Bill Heath for his considerable help with the history of the rose.

# The History of the Modern Rose

Up until the beginning of the 1800s the ancestors of the modern roses had barely evolved from the wild species. The ancient roses were cultivated by the first civilised nations who brought them from the wild to grow in their gardens. Their habit was lax and untidy, their petals few and their flowers short-lived. For centuries they continued with little change, other than a slight increase in number of petals due to preferential selection by the gardeners, and soon groups of roses became so fixed in their habit as to be later regarded as species.

The early European roses fell into five main groups: the gallicers, damasks, moss, albas and musks. Their main drawback was that they flowered only during the months of June and July. However, towards the end of the eighteenth century a revolution in rose-growing occurred, as roses from the Far East were crossed with the native European species and varieties that bloomed over a much longer period were soon developed. The first of this 'new blood' was brought back by merchant ships trading with India. Short thin-stemmed plants with small flowers discovered growing in Calcutta gardens were introduced to European gardeners to be grown as novelties. At first they were named Indica or Bengalese roses but it was later discovered that they were in fact the product of centuries of development by Chinese rose gardeners and more properly named *Rosa chinensis*. The most exciting feature of these new varieties was their remontant habit.

In 1792 the Royal Horticultural Society took delivery from the East India Company of a plant discovered by one of their plant collectors in Bengal. It was the semi-double crimson China rose, *Rosa chinensis semperflorens* or Slater's Crimson. In 1793 Parsons of Rickmansworth introduced to the European market a rose of similar habit but blush pink in colour which became known as the 'Old Blush China' or 'Parson's Pink China'.

Controlled hybridisation was not yet practised but the natural insect and wind pollination intermixed the ancient European species with the China blood and the local seedlings began to show traces of being remontant. When they became noticed amongst the damasks they were called hybrid damasks but because of the patronage of the Duchess of

Portland they soon became known as Portlands. Typically they retained the damask bloom but flowered over an extended period. The dark red blooms of Slater's Crimson China were unique in that they deepened with age instead of fading and were ultimately responsible for transmitting the deep red tones to the hybrids. 'Parson's Pink China' travelled to various parts of the world and there produced more hybrids which developed into families of their own (Bourbons, Noisettes, etc).

Demand for the new types of remontant roses encouraged nurserymen to plant out large numbers of them in open fields, and to collect and plant their seeds hoping that the seedlings would demonstrate an 'accidental' improved flowering plant. By re-selection plants improved in vigour, hardiness and flower size and by 1850 they had become known as hybrid perpetuals, a name that was by present-day standards very optimistic. They were often shy at producing late bloom, and most grew tall and leggy and had to be pegged down so that they would flower along the stem.

During the nineteenth century many Gentlemen's Gardening Societies existed to advance and promote horticulture. Most places held annual shows at which the gentry exhibited flowers and produce grown by their professional gardeners. It was not until the 1850s, however, that roses began to make an impact on the show bench and growers began to specialise in them, travelling with them to distant shows on the newly developed railway systems. One of these enthusiastic exhibitors was the Rev. S. Reynolds Hole, the vicar of Caunton, a small English village near Newark in Nottinghamshire. He decided that the rose was worth a show of its own, and acting as the enthusiastic secretary managed to stage the first ever National Rose Show in London on July 1 1858. Such was the beauty and amenability of the rose that the working classes also grew and cherished the rose on their tiny gardens and allotments. Just nine months after the first National Rose Show a more modest show, but one dedicated entirely to the rose, was staged at the General Cathcart Inn in St. Ann's Well Road, Nottingham. The Rev. Hole was asked to judge one of these early shows at Nottingham and wrote about it at length in his horticultural classic *A Book about Roses*.

Meanwhile in 1809 Hume's Blush Tea-scented China arrived from China, followed in 1824 by Parks Yellow Tea-scented China. These roses were classified as *Rosa odoratu*, and had flowers with larger petals than the hybrid perpetuals and opened from a pointed bud. Though the stems were thin for the size of the plant the leaves did match the size of the large flowers. Their scent resembled the scent of fresh tea leaves, hence the name 'tea-scented'. At first they were interbred solely as Tea roses and developed delicate fragrances, although the plants were delicate and needed the protection of glass against winter frosts. Although they were difficult to grow as garden roses, the beauty of the bloom was so admirable that they were persistently crossed with the hybrid perpetuals until a hardy rose tree was produced that would bear the classic shape of the tea. Open field pollination was the practice up until the 1850s when a few people began to appreciate that it was possible to transfer pollen between blooms by hand.

To the French must go the credit for the patronage and propagation of the early roses, as up to the 1870s they almost had a monopoly of new rose varieties. However, around this time an English farmer named Henry Bennett of Stapleford and Shepperton began to practise the controlled breeding of roses by adopting the type of records he used in his cattle breeding programme. In 1878 he sent out ten new varieties, all deliberately crossed with recorded parents, and called them 'Pedigree Hybrids of the Tea Rose'. His achievement was so impressive that in 1880 he was invited to speak to French rose-growers at Lyon, and though many were later to copy his ideas of controlled breeding he can truly be counted as the father of the hybrid tea.

'La France', raised in France in 1867, however, is regarded as the first authentic hybrid tea rose, although amazing as it may seem there was a resistance to these new roses by many horticulturalists who were determined to remain faithful to the old hybrid perpetuals. There was resistance to recognise them as a distinct new group and it was not until 1893 that the official body The National Rose Society relented and accepted them as a distinct type called the hybrid tea.

Henry Bennett's first ten roses were not too successful but the following year he raised a hybrid tea from 'Adam', a tea, and 'Xavier Olibo', a hybrid perpetual, and named it 'William Francis Bennett'. This he sold with the exclusive rights to America for 5,000 dollars. Three years later he sent out the famous 'Lady Mary Fitzwilliam', which also supplied the pollen for many other famous roses.

By 1900 the hybrid perpetuals were on their way out while hybrid teas were being bought in increasing numbers. By 1910 the exhibitors had altogether rejected the old pioneers of the rose and were showing the artificially bred hybrid teas which to this day reign supreme.

Controlled breeding had the advantage of the deliberate introduction of characteristics and improvements in size, health and colour.

One revolutionary change took place just before 1900 when no satisfactory yellow roses existed. Such as were in commerce were usually pale and faded to white in the sun. Pernet-Ducher, a French nurseryman, wondered if he could make a cross with a wild rose, the Persian Yellow, *Rosa foetida persiana,* which had bright, double, unfading yellow blooms during its once only summer flush. After hundreds of crosses between 1883 and 1888 he produced some seeds from the red hybrid perpetual 'Antonie Ducher' but it was not until 1893 that he noticed a self-set seedling with double blooms of orange-yellow which proved to be stable in colour, and furthermore remontant in habit. He named it 'Soleil d'Or', and from this he bred the first unfading yellow hybrid tea rose and named it 'Rayon d'Or', and the first true bicolour 'Juliet'. It is from this line of breeding called the pernetianas that came the modern flame-coloured roses.

Thus man and nature were to continue to produce the colourful modern hybrid tea, which might well be said to be the product of a wild rose and a persistent French breeder.

# The Story of Floribundas

The background of floribundas is slightly more involved than the history of the hybrid tea. Up to the 1950s bush roses that bloomed in clusters were called polyanthas or Poulsen roses. They derived from the crossing of a dwarf race of roses called polyantha pompons which produce clusters of small flowers with varieties of the hybrid tea. Poulsen of Denmark was the originator of the earliest of these crosses and he became famous for the range of bedding roses he developed. The taller and more popular varieties were all single, i.e. five-petalled, or semi-double, i.e. having two rows of petals. They were easy to cultivate and were very hardy, but rose-growers attempted and succeeded in introducing clusters of double roses that came to look more and more like a small hybrid tea bloom. So many varieties existed in the late 1950s that the purists objected to the name polyantha being applied to what clearly appeared to be a new strain of rose. Eventually a compromise was reached within the National Rose Society, which decided to term bedding varieties with a cluster flowering habit floribundas, whereas the name polyantha pompons was retained for the dwarfer habit smaller-flowering cluster roses.

A further complication arose when the American hybridists crossed the floribundas with the hybrid teas and obtained several large double flowers to the stem. The Queen Elizabeth rose is a good example of a type they called grandifloras. The Royal National Rose Society, however, prefers this class of rose to be called 'floribunda hybrid tea type'.

# Miniature Roses

It is impossible to divine the origin of the miniature rose but there are some interesting known facts that are recorded in history. The first modern instance of a miniature rose was a plant found on the tiny island of Mauritius in 1810. It was recorded as *Rosa chinensis minima* or 'Miss Lawrence's Rose'. Around this time a host of new plants were being discovered and, alas, its significance seems to have been overlooked. Much more widely known is the discovery in 1917 of a wonderful little rose that had been grown in alpine gardens for at least a century. It was brought to the notice of a local nurseryman by a Major Roulet who propagated cuttings of it and reintroduced it as *Rosa roulettii*.

*Rosa roulettii*, which grows to around 13 cm (5 in) high is bushy and has petite, perfectly formed double rose blooms, tiny thorns and leaves, is the ancestor of most of our modern miniature roses. It possesses the ability to impart its own miniature form to its progeny, and as the years advanced all sorts of roses were able to be dwarfed by this dominant characteristic. The first developments grew no taller than 13 cm (5 in) or so. 'Peon', 'Sweet Fairy' and Cinderella' were among the first seedlings to be introduced, and their use was restricted to pots, window boxes and rockeries. In recent years hybrid teas have been used in the breeding of new miniatures, and Meilland of France produced what is generally regarded as the perfect rose in miniature form, 'Starina'. Ralph Moore of California concentrated on the reduction in size of the moss rose, and after dedicating 40 years of his life to the project has produced a family of miniaturised moss roses, amongst them 'Dresden Doll'.

Modern miniature roses are easy to grow and are available in a wide range of attractive rose shades. The height of present-day varieties may be as tall as 30–38 cm (12–15 in) but they will grow almost anywhere without trouble. They will tolerate sun, rain and frost, and although they are generally grown out of doors they can be successfully reared in greenhouses and cold frames. Only with great difficulty, however, will they grow in the house. Although they are susceptible to all of the usual rose pests and diseases, many modern varieties show a marked resistance to 'mildew' and 'black spot'. The plants are best trimmed each season and 'pruned' only when they grow too large or top heavy.

# Classification

**Hybrid Tea**

Large shapely blooms usually produced in groups of three to the stem. It is common practice to remove the side buds so that all the vigour of the stem is directed into one flower of outstanding quality.

**Floribunda**

Several blooms to the stem. Flowers are usually double and long-lasting. Plants are used to create a massed bedding effect rather than for the production of beautiful individual blooms.

**Floribunda Hybrid Tea type (Grandiflora in the USA)**

Varieties in which the characteristics of both floribunda and hybrid teas are present. Some stems producing clusters of blooms and others fewer blooms but of more substance.

**Polyantha Pompon (Dwarf Polyantha)**

Bushes of dwarf habit bearing clusters of small blooms. One of the parents of the hybrid polyanthas.

**Hybrid Polyantha**

Now an almost obsolete term, the omnibus term floribunda having replaced it to embrace the original varieties and later introductions of a similar type. Such old varieties which are properly termed hybrid polyanthas are strong growing bush roses producing their single or semi-double blooms in clusters.

**Compacta**

A dwarf plant growing to around 30 cm (12 in) high. and, as the name implies, of a compact habit. Very free-flowering in clusters.

**Miniature**

Dainty roses that grow 13–38 cm (5–15 in) high. Flowers range from the miniature hybrid tea type

|  |  |
|---|---|
|  | to a full pompon. Suitable for pots, troughs and rockeries, and quite hardy out of doors. |
| Ground Cover | Low-growing plants that produce long prostrate fronds. Sometimes called miniature climbers, since they can be trained upwards to a limited degree. |
| Climber | Of upright climbing habit requiring support. Some varieties are raised as climbers, others as climbing sports of bush hybrid teas and floribundas. The most modern repeat-flowering climbers have an extended flowering period whereas the sports tend to have a spring and autumn flush of bloom. |
| Rambler | As the name implies, of rambling habit. Once used to cover large areas of open ground, the varieties in this group are best suited to covering fences, pergolas and trellises. Summer-flowering only and particularly prone to mildew and rust disease. |
| Shrub Roses | More properly termed hybrid musks, these are the result of crosses between the species *Rosa moschata* and various modern roses. The blooms, which often have a musk fragrance, are freely produced in early summer and intermittently for the rest of the season. They are excellent for hedging or in tall borders. |
| Hybrid Perpetual | Now an obsolete term, but used to describe the tall growing, mostly summer-flowering, parents of the modern hybrid tea. |
| Tea Roses | Thin-stemmed China roses, not hardy and requiring the protection of glass during the winter months. They have the fragrance of fresh tea leaves and are the source of fragrance and classic-shaped flowers in the modern hybrid tea. |

# *Explanation of Rose Terms*

| | |
|---|---|
| Basal shoot | A shoot emanating from the base of the plant. |
| Bedding | A somewhat ambiguous term as any variety might be used for bedding purposes, but generally applied to medium height varieties that produce a generous quantity of less than perfect blooms rather than a limited supply of immaculate specimens. |
| Bi-colour | A bloom composed of two colours. Usually the face of the petal contrasts with its reverse side. |
| Bud | A term applied to young unformed 'flower' buds and to the dormant 'eyes' concealed within the leaf shield formed at the union of the leaf system and the branch, according to context. |
| Budding | The term used in connection with propagation. It implies the operation of cutting a dormant 'bud' or 'eye' from the stem of a cultivated variety (the scion) and inserting it into an opening in the bark of an understock so that it will eventually replace the top growth of the understock with the cultivated variety. |
| Bush | The term used to describe any rose which grows, formally, within the 45–90 cm ($1\frac{1}{2}$–3 ft) height range. |
| Cut-back | Trees that have been pruned as distinct from trees in their first year which are known as 'maidens'. |
| Dead-heading | The removal of spent flower heads to stimulate the plant into flowering again. |

1 (previous page) Kilworth Gold  
3 Golden Times  

2 (opposite) ~~Wendy Cussons~~ APRICOT SILK  
4 Mischief ✓

5  Blue Moon

8  (opposite) Diorama

6  Isabel de Ortiz

7  Stephanie Diane

10 Polly Perkins

9 (opposite) Lovers' Meeting

11 Buccaneer

13 McGredy's Sunset

14 Monique

15 Christian Dior

16 Golden Giant

17 Troika
12 (opposite) Sunblest

18 Mayflower

19 (opposite) ~~Apricot Silk~~ WENDY CUSSONS  20 Pebble Mill

21 Lady Sylvia

22 Bettina

✓ 23 Alec's Red

24 Madame Henri Guillot

25 Souvenir de Jacques Verschuren

26 Mrs Sam McGredy

27 Royal Highness
✓ 28 (opposite) King's Ransom

30 Cover Girl

29 (opposite) Pink Favourite

31 Papa Meilland

32 Bonnie Scotland

33 Ruby Wedding

34 Ena Harkness

35 My Choice

36 André le Troquer

37 Harriny
38 (opposite) Sunsilk

40 Rose Gaujard

39 (opposite) Josephine Bruce

41 Mojave

42 Mister Lincoln

43 Dr A. J. Verhage

44 Pamela's Choice

45 Lily de Gerlache

46 Fragrant Cloud

47 Karl Herbst

48 Percy Thrower

49 Joyce Northfield

51 Serenade

52 The Doctor

53 Woman and Home

54 Virgo

55 Tzigane
50 (opposite) Dutch Gold

56 The Queen

57 Doreen

59 (opposite) Blessings

58 Alexander

61 Can Can

62 Spek's Yellow

63 Silver Wedding

✓ 64 Deep Secret

65 Sutter's Gold
60 (opposite) Lady Belper

66 Red Devil

67 Jean Rook

68 Sterling Silver

69 Stanley Gibbons

70 Julia's Rose

71 Whisky Mac

72 Leslie Johns

73 Woman's Realm

74 Amarillo

76 Silver Jubilee

75 (opposite) Piccadilly

77 Paris Match

78 Summer Holiday

79 Prima Ballerina

80 Stella

✓ 81 Peace

82 Champs Elysées

83 Super Star

84 (opposite) Dr John Snow

86 Montezuma

85 (opposite) Chicago Peace

87 Cheshire Life

88 Typhoon

89 Dr Albert Schweitzer

90 Royal Show

91 Panorama Holiday

92 Appreciation

93 McGredy's Yellow

94 Lord Louis

95 Lady Grade

97 John Waterer

98 Beauté

99 Message

100 Rosy Cheeks

101 Whisky Gill
96 (opposite) Gay Gordons

102 Grandpa Dickson

103 Perfecta

105 (opposite) Journey's End

104 Leslie G. Harris

107 Yellow Petals

108 Precious Platinum

109 Teneriffe

110 Vienna Charm

111 Corso
106 (opposite) Mullard Jubilee

112 Indian Chief

✓ 113 Just Joey

✓ 114 Ernest H. Morse

115 Princesse

116 Elizabeth Harkness

117 Young Quinn

118 Harlow

119 Invitation

120 Cock o' the North

121 (opposite) Westminster    122 Pascali

123 Vanda Beauty

124 Lady of the Sky

125 Duke of Windsor

126 Heart of England

129 (opposite) Queen Elizabeth

127 Garden Party

128 Lancastrian

130 Fleur Cowles

131 Dale Farm

132 Violet Carson

133 Gay Maid

134 Love Token

135 Orangeade

137 Masquerade

136 (opposite) Dearest

138 Golden Treasure

139 Hamburg Love

140 News

141 Picasso

142 Circus

143 Europeana

144 ~~Tonnerre~~ FASHION

145 ~~Fashion~~ TONNERRE

146 Vivacious

147 Coral Queen Elizabeth

148 Living Fire

149 Vilia

151 Baby Bio

150 (opposite) Spanish Orange

152 Marlena

153 Centrex Gold

154 Sarabande

155 Manx Queen

156 Doc

157 Topsi

158 Paprika

159 Orange Sensation

160 Charleston

161 Pink Parfait

163 (opposite) Arthur Bell

162 Jamboree

164 Iceberg

165 City of Leeds

166 King Arthur

167 Matangi

168 Frensham

169 Ama

170 Ma Perkins

171 Zambra

172 Coral Silk

173 Orange Silk

174 Evelyn Fison

175 My Girl

176 Rumba

177 (opposite) Glenfiddich

178 Allgold

179 Paddy McGredy

180 Anna Wheatcroft

181 City of Belfast

182 Margaret Merril

183 Goldmarie

184 Rob Roy

185 Sir Lancelot

186 Rosemary Rose

188 Iced Ginger

187 (opposite) Elizabeth of Glamis

189 Strawberry Fair

190 Goldgleam

191 Bengali

192 Lilli Marlene

193 Border Coral

194 Korona

195 Lavender Princess

196 (opposite) Tip Top    197 Ice White

198 Maria

199 Joseph's Coat

200 Dorothy Wheatcroft

201 Kassel

202 Lavender Lassie

203 Bonn

204 Chinatown

205 Köln am Rhein

206 Ballerina

207 Fred Loads

208 Climbing Iceberg

209 Climbing Fragrant Cloud

210 Compassion

211 Golden Showers

212 Danse du Feu

213 Aloha

214 Swan Lake

215 Climbing Blessings

216 Etude

217 Casino

218 Climbing Masquerade

219 Autumn Sunlight

220 Sympathie

221 Handel

222 Schoolgirl

223 Zephirine Drouhin

224 Pink Perpetue

225 Cherryade

226 Altissimo

227 Royal Gold

228 Kara

229 Dresden Doll

230 Fairy Magic

231 Lavender Jewel

232 Mood Music

233 Lemon Delight

234 Lavender Lace

235 Golden Angel

236 Peachy White

237 Sheri Anne

238 Strawberry Swirl

239 Green Diamond

240 Happy Thought

241 Andrea

242 Stacey Sue

243 Darling Flame

244 Over the Rainbow

245 Magic Carousel

246  Orange Honey

247  Stars 'n' Stripes

248  Scarlet Gem

249  Shakespeare Festival

250  Double Joy

251  Mary Marshall

252 Gypsy Jewel

253 Starina

254 Perle de Montserrat

255 Swedish Doll

256 Fire Princess

257 My Valentine

✓ 258 Little Flirt

259 Yellow Doll

260 Pour Toi

✓ 261 New Penny

262 Janice Tellian

263 Toy Clown

264  Beauty Secret

265  Rosina

266  June Time

267  Bambino

268  Gold Coin

269  Baby Darling

✓ 270 Sweet Fairy

271 Hula Girl

272 Judy Fischer

273 Dwarf King

274 Baby Gold Star

275 Eleanor

276 Born Free

277 Simple Simon

✓ 278 Baby Masquerade

279 Fashion Flame

280 Nozomi

281 Red Cascade

282 Coralin

283 Easter Morning

284 Rise 'n' Shine

285 Presumida

286 Rouletii

287 Cinderella

| | |
|---|---|
| Disbudding | The term used to describe the technique of removing the several subsidiary flower buds so as to direct all the vigour of the stem into the primary centre bloom. |
| Double blooms | Flowers consisting of 18–25 petals are so described. |
| Exhibition variety | A variety which because of the size and quality of its blooms is particularly favoured by rose judges. They usually possess many more petals than is desirable for a good all-weather garden rose. |
| Eye | A term used to describe the dormant shoot lying at the base of each leaf system. The point above which each stem is properly pruned. |
| Full petalled | A term applied to a rose bloom of substance. |
| Heeling in | A term which indicates temporary planting until the weather improves or new beds are ready to permit permanent planting. Bundles of trees are cut open and planted in a trench. Providing care is taken to cover the roots well with frost-free soil they will remain in good condition for several weeks. |
| Lateral growth | A shoot that emanates from an eye on a basal shoot. |
| Maiden | A rose bush that is up to one year old. The trees supplied by a rose nursery are 'maidens' having only one year's growth. |
| Pruning | The cutting off of part of the previous year's growth and atrophied stems to promote vigorous new flower stems. |
| Reversion | This term can be applied to a cultivated variety that has been outgrown by its understock, though it more generally refers to a variety that is a throwback to the variety of which it is a 'sport'. |
| Scion | The 'eyes' or 'buds' of the cultivated variety which are used when budding. |

| | |
|---|---|
| Seedling | A rose raised from seed. |
| Semi-double | A term applied to blooms having between five and fifteen petals, usually in a double row. |
| Shrub | A self-supporting plant that grows 1.2–1.5 m (4–5 ft) tall. Most suited for growing in borders. |
| Single-flowered | A bloom having one row of five petals only. |
| Sport | A term used to describe a mutation which concerns the altered colour of a variety while all the other characteristics remain the same as the parent plant. |
| Sport, climbing | A term used to describe a mutation which concerns the altered habit of a bush rose into a climber. A natural phenomenon which is usually noticed on nurseries where many thousands of a variety are grown. |
| Standard Rose or Tree Rose (USA) | A full standard rose used to be grafted or budded on to a 1.5 m (5 ft) high stem, and a half standard at 75 cm ($2\frac{1}{2}$ ft). Neither height was satisfactory and eventually a height of 1 m (3 ft) has become the universally accepted height at which to bud a hybrid tea or floribunda variety as a standard. |
| Standard Weeping | Sometimes called an umbrella rose. A rambler or climber grafted on to a stem so that the fronds weep downwards instead of growing upwards. |
| Stock | Also known as understock. This term is given to certain types of rose species that are selected as being most suitable upon which to bud cultivated varieties, the object being to obtain a more vigorous root action. |
| Union | This indicates the point of budding where the understock and cultivated variety are knitted together. |

# Notes on Cultivation

**Preparation of the Rose Bed**

Whatever the locality or type of soil, the fundamental consideration in the preparation of a rose bed is moisture. In most soils the supply of subterranean moisture is plentiful, therefore deep cultivation in the first instance is essential. In achieving this, it is important to remember to keep the fertile surface soil to the top, as the subsoil has little nutritive worth. It has, however, the valuable moisture-holding property ready to convert into soluble form the nourishment brought down by the rains from the fertile soil above.

The most satisfactory way to prepare a rose bed is by double trenching. First, take from one end of the bed a layer of topsoil about a spade's width and a spade's depth and transport it to the other end of the bed. The lower spit thus exposed is forked over, thoroughly broken up and then covered with a layer of manure. The next section of topsoil is then turned over to take the place of the soil that was removed and the next spit of subsoil is exposed for breaking up and manuring. The process is repeated until the end of the bed is reached and the topsoil removed from the first trench and put aside is used to cover the last. By working systematically you are ensured that the fertile topsoil remains on the top of the bed where it ought to be.

If the subsoil is clay mix into it a liberal quantity of hydrated lime when breaking it up. If the subsoil is light, sandy, gravelly or chalky the addition of organic material, peat, leaf mould or compost will be especially beneficial. All stable or farmyard manure that is used must be well rotted, and care must be taken that bare roots will not come into contact with neat manure or fertiliser used in the preparation of the rose beds. All preparation should be done well in advance of planting so as to allow a minimum of three weeks for the soil to settle.

**Arrival of Trees from the Nursery**

The importance of preventing the roots from drying out cannot be too strongly emphasised, as nothing in their after-care will remedy the damage so caused. When unpacking the bundle from the nursery, do so out of the wind. If it is not possible to plant them immediately, soak them and replace them in their package which should be placed in a cool, frost-proof place. It is not necessary to heel the roses in providing they can be planted within two weeks of their arrival and they are not permitted to dry out. If a longer interval before planting is contemplated, dig a trench sufficiently deep to cover the roots and a portion of the branches, open the bundle and lay the trees in a single row, crumble the soil over the roots and firm in with the heel to ensure that there are no air gaps in the soil. Laid-in trees will maintain their condition for up to three months, providing that the weather is cold enough to maintain their dormancy. As soon as signs of growth are noticed it is time that they were planted in their permanent positions.

### Planting

Mark out the position of each tree in the rose bed with a short cane. This ensures that the correct spacing is maintained throughout the planting operation. Bush trees are ideally spaced at 45 cm (18 in) apart in staggered rows that are themselves 45 cm (18 in) apart. A border of 30 cm (12 in) should be left between the bushes and the edge of the border. Miniature roses should be planted at 30 cm (12 in) apart and climbers need intervals of at least 1.8 m (6 ft) to allow them to spread properly. Open up a hole in the prepared ground of a good spade's width and depth, and place in it the roots of the tree so that the union of the scion with the rootstock is fractionally below the top of the soil. Spread the roots over as large an area as possible and then cover them with crumbled soil to which peat and a little bonemeal may be added. Firm with the hand to avoid air pockets and cover with more soil and tread lightly. Replace the remainder of the soil and firm with moderate pressure of the foot. When all is finished the union of the scion and rootstock should be just below the surface of the soil.

Container-grown roses can be planted at any time of the year. Care should be taken not to break the soil surrounding the root. Some containers are designed to rot away and can be planted along with the rose. Plastic and polythene pots must be carefully removed or they will restrict the root action of the plant.

### Feeding

There are two types of fertilisers: organic and inorganic. Organic fertilisers consist of material that has at some time lived as animal or vegetable and is in an advanced stage of decay. Examples are farmyard manure, bonemeal, garden compost, leaf mould, etc. Organics are used to increase the humus content of the soil, and they are long-lasting but slow-acting. Inorganic fertilisers are the raw chemical constituents of plant food such as nitrate of potash, sulphate of potash, etc. An example of an inorganic fertiliser would be a proprietary rose food. Inorganics are very quick-acting but are soon leached out of the soil.

Roses are best served by giving them a dressing of both types of fertiliser, a mulch of farmyard manure or a dressing of bonemeal in the early spring followed by two dressings of rose food in spring and in mid-summer. Since farmyard manure is difficult to come by a mixture of peat and bonemeal can be substituted to good effect.

## Pests and Diseases

Roses attract a number of parasitic organisms and insects that at the very least can mar the appearance of the plant and at worst kill it off altogether. Insect pests, such as aphids, caterpillars, thrip, leaf rolling sawflies and cockchafer beetles can be easily spotted, and even if there is some doubt as to their identity if they are causing harm they can easily be eliminated by modern 'systemic' insecticides. These are particularly effective against pests like the sawfly which induces the leaf to roll round its eggs and so protect them against conventional sprays.

All the diseases of the rose are fungus-related. Parasitic fungi spores are produced in great quantities and an attack can result in the defoliation and even the death of a plant. The most common disease is powdery mildew which attacks young immature shoots, shrivelling them and covering them with an unsightly white powdery substance. Black spot is the next most common disease in which the leaves are disfigured by large, round black spots before they eventually fall off. Rust is the worst of all the diseases of the rose, as it is a killer. The spores appear as rusty orange specks on the underside of the leaves. By mid-summer they have turned black and will be causing the tree to defoliate. Fortunately it is the least common of rose disorders. The best answer to all these problems is to search for varieties that show a definite resistance to the diseases and be ruthless in eliminating those that are troublesome year after year. There are several excellent spray preparations available today that are very potent in the control of fungus diseases. Following an attack the most successful treatment is to anticipate an attack next season and spray as a preventative before the symptoms show. Ask your garden supplier about the latest and best treatments, but take care, as some of the latest chemicals are not systemic and will wash off if it rains shortly after application.

# Pruning

There is no other gardening operation that is so controversial or that can cause so much confusion and distress, plunging ordinary intelligent people into impotent despair, as pruning. No wonder, perhaps, that so many articles are written and explanations are published, and arguments rage when every tree is different and no two seasons the same, so it is perhaps essential that we consider what kind of plant a rose is and how it behaves.

We are in the habit of calling our roses 'rose trees', which technically, of course, they are not. A tree concentrates all its efforts into producing a central trunk which bears branches and twigs. A rose sends up shoots from its base which will atrophy and die after a few years. These basal shoots are regularly replaced with a succession of new and vigorous branches, so that once established the bulk of the rose bush is maintained, indeed renovated.

Next we should consider the behaviour of a single basal shoot. In its first year it will grow and give a marvellous flower. If untouched, lesser flower stems will emanate from a point below the flowers, and in the following season still more shoots bearing significantly smaller blooms appear. The year after that these subsidiary shoots will bear stems with flowers of their own, though by now very poor in quality. When the vigour of the basal shoot is exhausted it will die back to around ground level. Pruning is done first of all to tame the rose to suit particular height requirements and then to 'short circuit' the growing cycle of the stem to prevent it from producing small insignificant growths. By obliging it to 'break' well down towards its base it behaves as if it were a fresh basal shoot and will bear another first class flower.

All that is really necessary is to know how to prune one shoot. As soon as the principle is grasped, it is simply a matter of applying it to each basal shoot (and shoots induced by previous pruning to behave as basal shoots) on the bush.

Let us assume that a newly planted bush has just one shoot. In the early spring cut this down to the nearest outward facing bud around 13 cm (5 in) from the crown (*see* p. 119), with clean, sloping cut just above the bud with really sharp secateurs. That first growing season it will

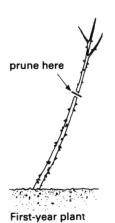
First-year plant

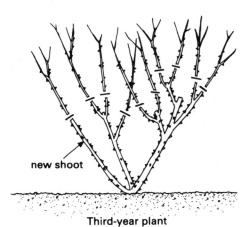
Third-year plant

Second-year plant

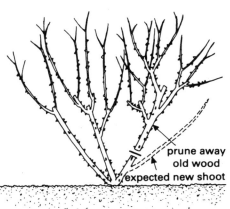
Four-year-old bush

branch from the bud to which you have pruned and probably produce a brand new basal shoot. The following spring prune back the basal shoot to the nearest outward facing bud around 13 cm (5 in) from the crown and the new growths from last year's stem to within about two buds of where they join the stem. The following year you will no doubt have gained another basal shoot, so prune it down to 13 cm (5 in). Prune back the growth on last year's basal shoot to within two buds of the shoot and tip back the branches of the three-year-old shoot to within 5 cm (2 in) of the previous year's pruning mark.

The fourth pruning acknowledges that the original shoot has given its best and though it will go on living for a year or two it is best cut off around 7.5 cm (3 in) from the base so that a new shoot may be induced to grow from a dormant bud lying in the crown of the bush. The rest of the bush should be cut back to within 5 cm (2 in) of the previous year's prunings.

## Summer Pruning
It is often a great worry to many gardeners to know just how much of the stem to remove when 'dead-heading'. The simplest guide is to feel down the stem of a tired, old bloom to a lump on its neck about 7.5 cm (3 in) away from the flower head. This is the point at which the ripened hip would eventually fall from the stem, and all that is needed is a nip of the fingers for the head to come away cleanly. If the bushes are growing vigorously you may prefer to take away the top 15 cm (6 in) of the stem and reduce the height of the second blooming. This operation requires that a sharp pair of secateurs be employed.

## Time to Prune
There is considerable argument as to the correct time to prune roses; should it be the autumn or spring? Both times are correct. You should reduce the height and bulk of the plants in the autumn so as to minimise wind damage, leaving the fine pruning until the springtime when it would seem that all the frosts are over and the new buds are just beginning to shoot.

## Pruning Miniatures
You do well to remember that modern miniature roses are closely related to some very tall vigorous roses so that half their nature is inclined to want to imitate the tall side of their family. It is best to regard miniatures as small shrub roses and simply trim them into shape until such time as they grow too large for their situation and only then prune them hard back. You may notice the occasional rogue shoot 'take off' and grow out

of all proportion to the rest of the bush. It is advisable to cut these extra long growths hard back, even in mid-summer, as it will not harm the plant but help maintain its dwarf habit.

### Ramblers and Climbers

A deal of confusion exists in distinguishing between ramblers and climbers. The true rambler produces annually from its base a number of slender pliable stems, whereas the climbers are less prolific and the fewer stems they send up are sturdy and stiff. Ramblers require to be thinned annually but since they flower on last year's wood this operation is best carried out just after the tree has bloomed so that the growth that follows will bear flower next season. The winter pruning of ramblers means that there will be fewer flowers the following summer.

Climbers need only the occasional thinning out. At some stage in their lives it may be necessary to cut away the whole of an atrophied basal shoot but only if there are younger growths already competing for growing room. Some hybrid tea sports take up to three years to produce flower during which time they do not require any pruning.

121

# Descriptions of Varieties

Numbers in brackets refer to colour plates.

c = Climbing    F = Floribunda    G = Grandiflora    HT = Hybrid Tea
M = Miniature    P = Polyantha    S = Shrub

**Alec's Red** (23)    HT
Raised by Cocker, Aberdeen, Scotland
Introduced 1973
*Parentage* Fragrant Cloud × Dame de Coeur
A deep cherry red with a rich and glorious perfume. The first rose to have won both the Royal National Rose Society's President's International Trophy Gold Medal and Edland Memorial Medal for fragrance. Blooms are of exhibition quality produced on strong stems that have no tendency to nod (a fault often associated with red hybrid teas). Medium height, upright.

**Alec's Red** (23)    C
A climbing sport of the bush HT. A vigorous variety that does not begin to flower for a season or more. Height 6 m (20 ft) or over. Not suitable for north walls.

**Alexander** (58)    HT
Raised by Harkness, Hertfordshire, England
Introduced 1972
*Parentage* Super Star × (Ann Elizabeth × Allgold)
An eye-catching orange vermilion with a delightful fragrance. Elegant bud shape and long stems make it a variety suitable for cutting. Care should be taken in siting this variety as its extraordinary vigour could prove an embarrassment. Bushes can grow to 1.5 m (5 ft) or more. Extra tall, upright.

**Allgold** (178)    F
Raised by LeGrice, Norfolk, England
Introduced 1958
*Parentage* Goldilocks × Ellinor LeGrice
Bright buttercup yellow with a modest fragrance. This is considered to be the first of the yellow floribundas capable of maintaining its deep shade well into maturity; previous introductions tended to pale and bleach. The first real yellow floribunda (as opposed to polyantha) to gain universal acceptance as a first class variety. Short compact habit.

**Aloha** (213)        C
Raised by Boerner, New York State, USA
Introduced 1949
*Parentage* Mercedes Gallart × New Dawn
Tawny and soft shell pink, reverse petals a deeper shade. Open blooms form tight rosette and last for a long while. Best grown against a low fence. Height 3–3.6 m (10–12 ft).

**Altissimo** (226)        C
Raised by Delbard-Chabert, Paris, France
Introduced 1966
*Parentage* Tenor × unknown
Bright crimson. With a single bloom composed of only seven petals and contrasting yellow stamens, this is the brightest red climber of all. The flowers are rather short-lived, but it has clusters of bloom and a repeat-flowering habit that makes up in quantity what the blooms lack in quality. Height up to 6 m (20 ft).

**Ama** (169)        F
Raised by Kordes, Holstein, Germany
Introduced 1955
*Parentage* Obergartner Wiebicke × Independence
Rich crimson-scarlet. A welcome introduction because although looking remarkably like the popular Frensham it exhibited a marked resistance to white powdery mildew, the curse of its predecessor. Bushes do not grow quite so rampant as Frensham but are sturdy, tidy plants. Medium height spreading.

**Amarillo** (74)        HT
Raised by Von Abrams, California, USA
Introduced 1961
*Parentage* Buccaneer × Lowell Thomas
Well-formed blooms of golden yellow. Large, well-shaped and surprisingly fragrant blooms were at its time of introduction most welcome. Previous deep yellow hybrid teas had been almost devoid of perfume. Bushes vigorous and upright with leathery light green foliage. Flower stems inclined to be a bit on the brittle side. Medium to tall, upright.

**Andrea** (241)        M
Raised by Moore, California, USA
Introduced 1978
*Parentage* Little Darling × unknown
Buds like small HTs. Carmine pink on the face of the petal silver on the reverse. Rather large blooms but a proportionately bushy plant. Grows to around 30 cm (1 ft).

**André le Troquer** (36)        HT
Raised Meilland, Cap d'Antibes, France
Introduced 1946
*Parentage* unknown
Orange and apricot shades that show off to best advantage in the mild UK summers. Amongst the

123

first post-war hybrid tea introductions from Meilland that were to set new standards for hybrid teas, here were pastel shades, elegance and extraordinary fragrance combined. Medium height, spreading.

**Anna Wheatcroft** (180)  F
Raised by Tantau, Holstein, Germany
Introduced 1958
*Parentage* Cinnabar seedling × unknown
Pale vermilion. A very delicate yet striking floribunda which had but a single row of petals with which to catch the eye. It is remarkable that this variety managed to become so popular as its style was contrary to the then current trend towards a more double and long-lasting flower form. Bushes are very vigorous and produce large clusters of bloom and dark glossy foliage. Medium height, spreading.

**Appreciation** (92)  HT
Raised by Gregory, Nottingham, England
Introduced 1971
*Parentage* Queen Elizabeth × Super Star
Shades of vermilion. An attractive if somewhat undistinguished rose the parentage of which led one to think it was destined to become a noteworthy variety. In spite of its vigour it proved to be very susceptible to black spot and was withdrawn from commerce before it might gain a popular following. Tall, upright.

**Apricot Silk** (19)  HT
Raised by Gregory, Nottingham, England
Introduced 1965
*Parentage* Souvenir de Jacques Verschuren × Cover Girl
Apricot shades. A much sought-after yet extremely rare colour in modern roses, a shade that shows off to best advantage in the more modest UK summers. Too much sun and these pastel shades bleach to an unattractive parchment. Buds are extremely slender of form, in perfection they are the most elegant the rose has yet produced. Bushes are vigorous but are best only lightly pruned as the plants are most productive when they reach a height of around 1.2 m (4 ft). Tall upright habit.

**Arthur Bell** (163)  F
Raised by McGredy, Auckland, New Zealand
Introduced 1965
*Parentage* Clare Grammerstorf × Piccadilly
Deep clear yellow in the bud, pales when fully open. Blooms are like small hybrid tea buds, double and produced in large sprays. An unusual feature is its pronounced fragrance, seldom found in yellow roses and even rarer in a floribunda. The dainty bud form makes it popular with flower arrangers. Bushes are healthy and vigorous with lots of glossy light

green foliage. Medium height, upright.

**Arthur Bell** (163)     C
A climbing sport of the floribunda. Once established it has two distinct flowering periods, spring and autumn, with only a few intermittent flowers in between. The colour fades too quickly but the fragrance is a compensation. Height around 4.5 m (15 ft).

**Autumn Sunlight** (219)     C
Raised by Gregory, Nottingham, England
Introduced 1965
*Parentage* Spectacular × Climbing Goldilocks
Orange vermilion. Semi-globular blooms that hang in clusters. Sweetly scented with an apple-like fragrance. A repeat-flowering habit with regular bloom production after the main spring flush. Bright green glossy foliage and a free growing habit. Height 3.6–4.5 m (12–15 ft).

**Baby Bio** (151)     F
Raised by E. Smith, Nottingham, England
Introduced 1977
*Parentage* Golden Treasure × unnamed seedling
Bright golden yellow, rosette-shaped blooms in great profusion. They cover the bush which is a short, sturdy and compact-growing plant. There has been much discussion as to what to call this type of rose; 'cushion roses' or 'patio roses' would seem to describe them best. As gardens become smaller so the dwarf habit embodied in this variety seems to become more popular. Growth is to around 45 cm (1½ ft). Plant at 45 cm (1½ ft) spacing for a continuous ribbon effect. Short compact habit.

**Baby Darling** (269)     M
Raised by Moore, California, USA
Introduced 1964
*Parentage* Little Darling × Magic Wand
Coral and apricot. Dainty little buds in soft pastel shades. Very free-flowering and trouble-free plants around 30 cm (1 ft) tall.

**Baby Doll** See **Tip Top**     F

**Baby Gold Star** (274)     M
Raised by Dot, Barcelona, Spain
Introduced 1940
*Parentage* Eduardo Toda × Rouletii
Golden yellow. Flat rosette-shaped blooms formed of tiny ruffled petals clustered round the centre of the bloom to conceal the stamens. Vigorous plants which grow to around 25 cm (10 in).

**Baby Masquerade** (278)     M
Raised by Tantau, Holstein, Germany
Introduced 1956
*Parentage* Tom Thumb × Masquerade
Yellow, pink and red. The blooms change colour from a light yellow

bud into a rose red open flower. Intensity of colour depends upon the amount of sunshine. A vigorous plant growing upwards of 30 cm (1 ft).

**Ballerina** (206)                    S
Raised by Bentall, Essex, England
Introduced 1937
*Parentage* unknown
Light pink with a white eye. Small blooms around 2.5 cm (1 in) across form in dainty hydrangea-like trusses. This variety is a hybrid musk and possesses a musk fragrance. The bushes have a repeat-flowering habit and give a good show of bloom all summer long. Suitable for borders, even herbaceous borders, where they can grow to over 1 m (3 ft) high.

**Bambino** (267)                    M
Raised by Dot, Barcelona, Spain
Introduced 1953
*Parentage* a sport of Perle de Alcanada
Deep rose pink. One of the smallest miniatures. The bloom is not much bigger than 1.3 cm ($\frac{1}{2}$ in) across and the plants grow from 15 to 25 cm (6–10 in). Ideal for alpine rockeries.

**Beauté** (98)                    HT
Raised by Mallerin, Isere, France
Introduced 1953
*Parentage* Mme Joseph Perrand × unnamed seedling
Light orange. Long urn-shaped buds. Broad reflexing petals—not too many so as to spoil its most elegant form. A very suitable variety for cutting as its blooms are held individually on sturdy flower stems. Also an excellent bedding variety as its habit is to spread and fill up the space between bushes rather than leave it bare. One of the first orange shades to show a resistance to powdery mildew. Medium bushy habit.

**Beauty Secret** (264)                    M
Raised by Moore, California, USA
Introduced 1965
*Parentage* Little Darling × Magic Wand
Cardinal red with a white flushed carmine reverse. A big bloom that rather loses its form after the early bud shape, which can reach up to 3.8 cm ($1\frac{1}{2}$ in) across. Plants are also on the large side growing to 38 cm (15 in) high or more. One of the most fragrant miniatures.

**Bengali** (191)                    F
Raised by Kordes, Holstein, Germany
Introduced 1969
*Parentage* Dacapo × unknown seedling
An attractive confection of shades of orange and gold. Small perfectly-shaped buds have an attraction for the flower arranger in search of scaled-down fragrant orange coloured roses. Plants are bushy yet compact and dressed in dark green foliage and deliver a good quantity of bloom in big

flower trusses all season long. Medium height grower.

**Bettina** (22)     HT
Raised by Meilland, Cap d'Antibes, France
Introduced 1953
*Parentage* Peace × (Mme Joseph Perraud × Demain)
Orange shaded through pink. Cup-shaped fragrant blooms retain a tight centre when the outer petals have opened to form a full bloom. A feature of the flower is to turn more towards salmon rather than bleach in strong sunshine. Bushes have dark glossy bronze-green foliage and have a spreading habit so are good for cutting and bedding alike. Medium height grower.

**Blessings** (59)     HT
Raised by Gregory, Nottingham, England
Introduced 1967
*Parentage* Queen Elizabeth × unknown
An almost translucent shade of soft coral-pink. Buds are shapely, pleasingly fragrant and are held in clusters. A seedling of the Queen Elizabeth rose, it inherits just the right amount of vigour from its parent so as to be robust without being overpoweringly tall. Flowers tend to be held in neat clusters towards the top of the bush. Growth is healthy and disease-free. Planting distance should not be more than 50 cm (20 in) apart for good ground cover as growth tends to be more upwards than outwards. Tall upright grower.

**Blessings** (215)     C
A climbing form of the bush HT. The fragrance of the blooms seems to be more pronounced in the climbing form, perhaps because there is a greater concentration of flowers. A very vigorous plant that can take at least two years to become properly established. Height 6–7.5 m (20–25 ft).

**Blue Moon** (5)     HT
Raised by Tantau, Holstein, Germany
Introduced 1964
*Parentage* Sterling Silver seedling × unknown
Also known as Mainzer Fastnacht. This was reckoned to be the first 'blue' rose, though to be more accurate the colour is more like a lilac. A great achievement, nevertheless, as this was surely the best grower of all of this shade (including its forerunner and part parent 'Sterling Silver' which although pretty lacked real vigour). Fragrance and long flower stems add to the charm and make it irresistible to flower arrangers in search of the unusual. Medium upright grower.

**Bonn** (203)     S
Raised by Kordes, Holstein, Germany
Introduced 1950
*Parentage* Hamburg × Independence

Orange scarlet. Rather loose double blooms, the lack of quality, however, being compensated for by the generosity of the cluster and the freedom of flowering of the shrub. This variety might well be regarded as the first of the 'modern' shrub roses. Unlike the old-fashioned species this type of Kordes-raised shrub flowers throughout the summer, just like a floribunda; and furthermore they can be winter pruned without subsequent loss of bloom. Bushes will grow, self-supporting, up to 1.5 m (5 ft) high.

**Bonnie Scotland** (32)  HT
Raised by Anderson, Aberdeen, Scotland
Introduced 1976
*Parentage* Wendy Cussons × Percy Thrower
Fragrant deepest pink set against dark glossy foliage incline one to the view that this is the best pink in commerce today. A cross between the damask-perfumed Wendy Cussons and the crisp-petalled Percy Thrower. A really hardy Scottish-raised variety, proof against the worst of wind and weather. Medium height bushes give a repeat-flowering performance throughout the season.

**Border Coral** (193)  F
Raised by de Ruiter, Hazerswoude, Holland
Introduced 1957
*Parentage* Signal Red × Fashion

Rich coral pink. A best seller of the 1960s when the demand was for a more double form of the floribunda. Few of its contemporaries had the shape or quantity of petals that this variety possessed, let alone were able to match it for health and vigour. Here also was a most welcome colour break which introduced pastel shades into the range of floribundas. Medium bushy habit.

**Born Free** (276)  M
Raised by Moore, California, USA
Introduced 1978
*Parentage* Red Pinocchio × Little Chief
Orange red. A semi-double bloom that opens to show bright yellow stamens. Buds are not really elegant, so the beauty of the plant lies in the quantity of bloom it produces rather than the quality. Plants growing to around 38 cm (15 in).

**Buccaneer** (11)  HT
Raised by Swim, California, USA
Introduced 1952
*Parentage* Golden Rapture × (Max Krause × Capt. Thomas)
Buttercup yellow. Good clear colour in both bud and mature flower. This was the first significant step forward from Spek's Yellow in the search for an unfading golden yellow garden rose. It has a drawback in that it is a very tall grower often unable to provide adequate support for its 'lanky' top growth. Plants grow in

untidy fashion often over 1.2 m (4 ft) tall.

**Can Can** (61)                      HT
Raised by Le Grice, Norfolk, England
Introduced 1958
*Parentage* Just Joey × (Mischief × Superior)
Orange flame. Loosely-formed buds in an eye-catching shade of orange flushed gold are produced early in the season and borne very freely on a vigorous but short-growing bush. The blooms are large in relation to the bush and are very fragrant. Bushes do not grow much higher than 45 cm (18 in) and are clothed in healthy glossy foliage.

**Casino** (217)                      C
Raised by McGredy, Auckland, New Zealand
Introduced 1963
*Parentage* Coral Dawn × Buccaneer
Deep yellow in the bud, soft yellow when fully open. Fragrant, hybrid tea shaped blooms, the deepest yellow repeat-flowering climber and certainly the best formed buds. Other yellows tend to lose their shape. Height 3.6–4.5 m (12–15 ft).

**Centrex Gold** (153)                 F
Raised by Smith, Nottingham, England
Introduced 1975
*Parentage* Alison Wheatcroft × Chinatown

Pale golden yellow. A full, double bloom with an arrangement of twenty-five or so petals that contrive to conceal the centre of the bloom. Trusses of flower are very big and the bushy plant possesses a free-blooming habit. Medium height bushes clothed in mid-green, matt foliage.

**Champs Elysées** (82)                HT
Raised by Meilland, Cap d'Antibes, France
Introduced 1957
*Parentage* Monique × Happiness
Rich crimson petals with a velvet-like texture. Petite blooms weather well in inclement UK summers. Although no doubt introduced as the brightest red HT then available it possessed a reasonable perfume. There followed a long period when many bright red roses totally lacked fragrance but hereafter the gardener would not have to suffer red roses that turned blue as they aged. Bushes were sturdy but short. Low, compact habit.

**Charleston** (160)                   F
Raised by Meilland, Cap d'Antibes, France
Introduced 1963
*Parentage* Masquerade × (Radar × Caprice seedling)
A more double form of the colourful Masquerade, one of its parents. The bud form is mostly yellow tinged pink but the open bloom reacts to sunlight so that the red pigments become dominant. These

ever-changing colours make for a most attractive bush. The buds resemble small hybrid tea blooms. The mature blooms are semi-double and contrast with a row of bright yellow stamens.

**Cherryade** (225)                              C
Raised by de Ruiter, Hazerswoude, Holland
Introduced 1961
*Parentage* New Dawn × Red Wonder
Redcurrant pink to cherry red. Big, fragrant, open blooms set against dark green glossy foliage. A semi-climber or shrub rose not able to grow much taller than 2.4 m (8 ft). Repeat-flowering habit. In spite of its somewhat 'old fashioned' open flower style, it makes a fine pillar rose.

**Cheshire Life** (87)                          HT
Raised by Fryer, Knutsford, England
Introduced 1972
*Parentage* Prima Ballerina × Princess
Brilliant vermilion-orange. Neat and tidy blooms with an unusual spiral bud formation. There is a host of vermilion roses, each one striving for the title of best orange rose ever, and this must be regarded as one of the finest. Strong, vigorous disease-free bushes can outgrow the unwary gardener. A variety for the back row of a border. Very tall upright habit.

**Chicago Peace** (85)                          HT
Introduced by Conrad-Pyle, Pennsylvania, USA
Introdyced 1962
*Parentage* a sport of Peace
A colourful sport of the famous Peace rose discovered, by chance, in the garden of a Chicago rose grower. It looks so different that it may well deceive as to its origin. Petals have a rich copper outer edge and a phlox-pink base. The depth of colour in the mature bloom is somewhat dictated by the amount of sunshine it receives. The plant embodies all the superlative growing qualities of its remarkable parent. Tall vigorous grower.

**Chinatown** (204)                              S
Raised by Poulsen, Kvistgaard, Denmark
Introduced 1963
*Parentage* Columbine × Clare Grammerstorf
Also known as Ville de Chine. Golden yellow sometimes edged pink. A flat, rosette-shaped bloom held on long stiff stems in clusters of three to five blooms. The habit of the bush is to grow fresh upright stems each season so that the plants can be pruned down to around 45 cm (18 in) each winter. The blooms are exceptionally fragrant for a yellow rose. Self-supporting growth of up to 1.5 m (5 ft) high can be expected from trees planted in a sheltered border.

130

**Christian Dior** (15) HT
Raised by Meilland, Cap d'Antibes, France
Introduced 1958
*Parentage* (Independence × Happiness) × (Peace × Happiness)
Rich scarlet, flushed crimson. A bloom of poise and elegance as befits a rose that bears the name of the famous fashion designer. The flowers are symmetrical and full with petals regular and reflexed. The rich colour lasts from bud to maturity. Blooms are held erect on strong, stout stems which give an indication as to the healthy and vigorous habit of the bush. Medium height grower.

**Cinderella** (287) M
Raised by de Vink, Boskoop, Holland
Introduced 1953
*Parentage* Cecile Brunner × Tom Thumb
White tinged pale pink. Tiny buds opening to full, long-lasting rosette-shaped blooms. Inclined to mark in wet weather. Small, bushy plants in scale with rockery plants can be kept down to neat round 25-cm (10-in) high plants.

**Circus** (142) F
Raised by H. Swim, California, USA
Introduced 1956
*Parentage* Fandango × Pinocchio
Orange pink and yellow. Often described as a muted version of the colourful Masquerade, although it is interesting to note that it is not related. Blooms are full and double with more petals than a good many hybrid teas and are held in nicely separated clusters. Outstanding in its year of introduction for its generous production of long-lasting, colourful flowers for which quality it won many awards. Bushes are tidy growers. Medium height grower.

**City of Belfast** (181) F
Raised by McGredy, Auckland, New Zealand
Introduced 1968
*Parentage* Evelyn Fison × (Circus × Korona)
Bright, glowing red. Rosette-shaped buds last a long while to give a good continuous show throughout the season. Medium height bushes have an abundance of glossy foliage and a constitution that won for the variety the Gold Medal of the Royal National Rose Society.

**City of Leeds** (165) F
Raised by McGredy, Auckland, New Zealand
Introduced 1966
*Parentage* Evelyn Fison × (Spartan × Red Favourite)
Rich clear salmon. Tidy dainty HT type buds held in large clusters. The centre bloom can be relied upon to open first and develop a bloom of some 9 cm ($3\frac{1}{2}$ in) across. The rest of the truss follows with a burst of colour from four or five supplementary buds. A vigorous and upright grower up to 1 m (3 ft)

tall with plentiful dark green glossy foliage. Provides lots of bloom for bedding and even occasional cutting. The most outstanding salmon pink floribunda ever introduced. Medium upright grower.

**Cock o' the North** (120)    HT
Raised by Cocker, Aberdeen, Scotland
Introduced 1974
*Parentage* Ernest H. Morse × unnamed seedling
Bright crimson red. A fragrant red rose that the northern rose growers can crow about. This rose was developed to suit chilly conditions and was bred and tested on the windswept hills around Aberdeen. The colder the season the more spectacular the blooms. Too much sunshine results in insignificant, diminutive flowers. Growth is strong and sturdy and flower stems stout and upright. Medium upright grower.

**Compassion** (210)    C
Raised by Harkness, Hertfordshire, England
Introduced 1972
*Parentage* White Cockade × Prima Ballerina
A blend of salmon pink, orange and apricot. Petite double blooms with a strong sweet fragrance. A feature of this climber is its dark, leathery foliage, glossy and disease-resistant. Suited to north walls. Height 3–3.6 m (10–12 ft).

**Coralin** (282)    M
Raised by Dot, Barcelona, Spain
Introduced 1955
*Parentage* Mephisto × Perla de Alcanada
Deep coral pink. A rather large bloom for a miniature that is formed of around forty petals. Plants are also on the large side, and need to be pruned hard if they are to retain their miniature status. A good, 'grow anywhere' plant. 38–50 cm (15–20 in) high.

**Coral Queen Elizabeth** (147)    F
Raised by Gregory, Nottingham, England
Introduced 1966
*Parentage* Queen Elizabeth × unknown
Deep coral salmon. So dominant were the form and character of the Queen Elizabeth rose in this seedling that it seemed proper to nominate it as a coral version. The buds were rather tighter and more conical than those of the parent, though the growth is similar in all other respects. Tall and vigorous grower.

**Coral Silk** (172)    F
Raised by Gregory, Nottingham, England
Introduced 1972
*Parentage* Pink Parfait × unknown
Coral peach. Full rosette-shaped blooms held in large trusses do not reveal their stamens until the last stages of maturity. Soft gentle colours that refuse to fall out with

any other shade of rose in the garden. Its bushy habit makes it especially suitable for bordering paths and lawns. Medium compact grower.

**Corso** (111)  HT
Raised by Cocker, Aberdeen, Scotland
Introduced 1976
*Parentage* Anne Cocker × Dr. A.J. Verhage
Orange vermilion. Of special interest to the flower arranger because this rose was the result of selection and development in search for long-lasting cutting roses. Classical urn-shaped blooms have firm, crisp petals, tightly wrapped, and are reckoned to last up to fourteen days in water. Growth is healthy and vigorous, bushes repeatedly producing long straight stems ideal for cutting. Bushes grow to around 1 m (3 ft) high. Tall vigorous habit.

**Cover Girl** (30)  HT
Raised by Von Abrams, California, USA
Introduced 1960
*Parentage* Sutters Gold × (Mme Henri Guillot × seedling)
Burnt orange and gold. Lovely urn-shaped buds open to high centred blooms. There is a deep copper veining etched on to the upper face of the petal whereas the reverse side is a tone or two lighter. Bushes are compact upright growers that can be kept at around 60 cm (2 ft) high. An ideal

bedding rose with a modest fragrance. Short upright habit.

**Dale Farm** (131)  F
Raised by E. Smith, Nottingham, England
Introduced 1973
*Parentage* Vera Dalton × Wendy Cussons
Rich, clear salmon. Flowers open like small hybrid tea buds and develop in clusters to full blooms over 7.5 cm (3 in) across. An impressingly clear colour for mass bedding effect. A strong upright grower, 75 cm–1 m (2½–3 ft) high, producing many flower stems with large clusters of moderately fragrant blooms. Disease-free, sound and healthy. Medium upright habit.

**Danse du Feu** (212)  C
Raised by Mallerin, Isere, France
Introduced 1953
*Parentage* Paul's Scarlet Climber × unnamed seedling
Also known as Spectacular. Scarlet red double blooms open to 'dusty' orange-red. Flowers held in small clusters. The first of the repeat-flowering climbing roses which gave recurrent flower production throughout the season rather than a spectacular spring and autumn show. Height 3–3.6 m (10–12 ft).

**Darling Flame** (243)  M
Raised by Meilland, Cap d'Antibes, France
Introduced 1971

133

*Parentage* (Rimosa × Josephine Wheatcroft) × Zambra

Orange red and gold. A cheerful bi-colour, the paler reverse contrasting with the orange face of the petals. One of the brightest miniatures supported by robust sturdy little bushes growing to around 30 cm (1 ft) high.

**Dearest** (136)                                F

Raised by A. Dickson, Co. Down, N. Ireland

Introduced 1960

*Parentage* unnamed seedling × Spartan

Soft 'geranium lake' pink. Blooms often as much as 7.5 cm (3 in) across are double in form and very sweetly scented. The clearest, softest pink which does not show its stamens so as to give the impression of being full blown, nor does it fade to an unattractive bleached white. Big clusters of bloom clothe the whole bush from top to bottom. Indeed it would be no exaggeration to nominate Dearest as the best soft pink floribunda ever. Bushy medium height plants.

**Deep Secret** (64)                             HT

Raised by Tantau, Holstein, Germany

Introduced 1977

*Parentage* unknown

Also known as Mildred Scheel. Dark crimson. Petals have the texture of velvet, the outermost being almost black, the inner heart a lighter crimson red. As fragrant as one might ever expect a deep red rose to be. The bushes have healthy dark green foliage and it is good to note that they are not prone to mildew attack, the curse of most other 'black' roses. Medium upright habit.

**Diorama** (8)                                  HT

Raised by de Ruiter, Hazerswoude, Holland

Introduced 1965

*Parentage* Peace × Beauté

Apricot yellow, the outermost petals tinged with orange. High centred blooms 10–12.5 cm (4–5 in) across. Remarkably fragrant for a yellow rose. Vigorous bushes grow on the tall side and are clothed in dark green foliage. Blooms, produced in clusters, weather well and make for an ideal bedding rose, disbudded. The flowers are suitable for cutting or exhibition work. Tall, spreading habit.

**Doc** (156)                                    P

Raised by de Ruiter, Hazerswoude, Holland

Introduced 1954

*Parentage* Robin Hood × unnamed seedling

Phlox pink. Small semi-double blooms that smother a diminutive bush. Doc is chosen to represent the range of dwarf growing polyantha varieties known as Compacta roses. They grow no taller than 45 cm (18 in) high and are easily trained to edge paths to give a continuous low hedge effect. There were seven varieties introduced and named after the seven dwarfs: Doc phlox pink, Bashful deep rose pink, Dopey crimson, Grumpy soft pink, Happy currant red, Sleepy bright rose pink and Sneezy single, soft pink. Short compact growers.

**Doreen** (57)                          HT
Raised by Robinson, Hinckley, England
Introduced 1951
*Parentage* Lydia × McGredy's Sunset
Golden orange flushed scarlet. Each petal reflexes sharply to give a unique spiky effect to the bloom. For many years after its introduction it remained the brightest golden bedding rose of all. The habit of the bush is to be rather untidy, a fault which is easily forgiven in view of its extreme generosity in flower production. Low spreading habit.

**Dorothy Wheatcroft** (200)      s
Raised by Tantau, Holstein, Germany
Introduced 1960
*Parentage* unknown
Orange scarlet. Semi-double flowers with a centre of bright yellow stamens. A tall trouble-free vigorous shrub with large clusters of bloom. A Royal National Rose Society Gold Medal variety, which award testifies as to its health and vigour. The open style of bloom is not in the current vogue nor yet is its tall habit suited to most modern

suburban gardens. Grows over 1.2 m (4 ft) high.

**Double Joy** (250)                    M
Raised by Moore, California, USA
Introduced 1979
*Parentage* Little Darling × New Penny
Peachy pink. Tubular-shaped buds opening to full double blooms, some of the largest seen on miniature roses, around 3.8 cm ($1\frac{1}{2}$ in) across. Named because it has a fragrance to match its looks. Plants grow to around 30 cm (12 in) tall.

**Dr A.J. Verhage** (43)              HT
Raised by Verbeek, Aalsmeer, Holland
Introduced 1963
*Parentage* Tawny Gold × (Baccara × seedling)
Apricot yellow. A characteristic of this variety is an attractive frill along the outer edge of each petal. Its fragrance, clarity and depth of colour together with its repeat-flowering habit ensured that it was well represented at the Aalsmeer Flower Market and consequently in the florist's shop as a cut flower. The plant usually has a slow start and is much better as a two-year-old 'cut back' but once established it is a normal healthy bush. Medium height plants.

**Dr Albert Schweitzer** (89)      HT
Raised by Delbard-Chabert, Paris, France
Introduced 1961

*Parentage* Chic Parisien × Michele Meilland
Pale pink with a rose red reverse. Some thirty-five very large petals contribute to a somewhat loose unshapely bloom. A variety that prefers a warm dry climate as the petals tend to gum together in their early bud form in wet weather. The bushes, however, are very vigorous and free-flowering with a vigorous upright constitution and leather-like broad glossy foliage.

**Dresden Doll** (229)                     M
Raised by Moore, California, USA
Introduced 1975
*Parentage* Fairy Moss × unnamed moss seedling
Shell pink. A cup-shaped bloom enclosing a ring of yellow stamens. A miniaturised moss rose that took the raiser over forty years to develop. A feature of the plant is the 'mossy' buds and stems. 30–45 cm (12–18 in) high plants give continuous bloom all season.

**Dr John Snow** (84)                     HT
Raised by Gandy, Rugby, England
Introduced 1979
*Parentage* Helen Traubel × unnamed seedling
Creamy white. An exquisitely shaped rose possessing a lovely fragrance. This rose is named as a tribute to the man who developed the use of ether for anaesthetic purposes. Large exhibition type blooms are prone to weather damage and should be shielded throughout their development if destined for the show bench. Bushes have a spreading rather than upright habit. Medium bushy grower.

**Duftwolke**                     HT
See **Fragrant Cloud**

**Duke of Windsor** (125)                     HT
Raised by Tantau, Holstein, Germany
Introduced 1969
*Parentage* unknown
Also known as Herzog von Windsor. Brilliant, clear orange vermilion. Small petite buds held singly or in clusters. A very sweet apple-like fragrance. A compact bushy grower to about 60 cm (2 ft) and very free-flowering, which habit suits it for short, tidy borders. Alas, there is a grave flaw in its constitution: it is very prone (in the UK especially) to mildew attack and if you grow this variety you need to spray regularly to ward off the disfiguring blemishes of the disease.

**Dutch Gold** (50)                     HT
Raised by Tysterman, Wisbech, England
Introduced 1978
*Parentage* Peer Gynt × Whisky Mac
Deep golden yellow that does not fade as the blooms open. Very shapely full blooms are fragrant and are unusually weather-resistant for their size. The plants are very healthy, sturdy and

strong growers to around 1 m (3 ft) tall, clothed in light green glossy foliage. The blooms are inclined to turn pink rather than bleach as they develop, indicating a strong Peace influence somewhere in its breeding.

**Dwarf King** (273)　　　　　M
Raised by Kordes, Holstein, Germany
Introduced 1957
*Parentage* World's Fair × Tom Thumb
Crimson red. A rather flat bloom around 3.8 cm (1½ in) across with inner petals that conceal the heart of the bloom even when it is fully open. Delicately fragrant. Inclined to mildew in a wet season. Small, round plants grow up to 25 cm (10 in) high.

**Easter Morning** (283)　　　　M
Raised by Moore, California, USA
Introduced 1960
*Parentage* Golden Glow × Zee
Ivory white. Small cabbage-like blooms formed of petals that fold back and maintain a shapely appearance even when fully open. A good exhibition variety if carefully protected from weather damage with something in the order of sixty petals worth of quality in the 3.8 cm (1½ in) blooms. Vigorous, bushy plants can fill out to around 30 cm (1 ft) cushions.

**Eleanor** (275)　　　　　　M
Raised by Moore, California, USA

Introduced 1960
*Parentage* (*R. wichuraiana* × Floradora) × (seedling × Zee)
Coral pink. Cup-shaped blooms in a clear delicate pastel shade. A good variety for cut bloom. Repeat-flowering plants growing to around 30 cm (1 ft) high. Healthy leathery foliage.

**Electron**　　　　　　　　HT
See **Mullard Jubilee**

**Elizabeth Harkness** (116)　　HT
Raised by Harkness, Hertfordshire, England
Introduced 1969
*Parentage* Red Dandy × Piccadilly
Cream tinted buff with touches of rosy amber revealed as the bloom opens. Wide, shapely flowers composed of petals with an acute reflex which tend to exaggerate the high centre of the bloom. Fast-growing bushes can produce hosts of exhibition quality blooms as well as possessing a first class bedding habit. Unlike most pastel pink roses it shows a determined resistance to weather damage.

**Elizabeth of Glamis** (187)　　F
Raised by McGredy, Auckland, New Zealand
Introduced 1964
*Parentage* Spartan × Highlight
Clear coral salmon with a golden base to each petal. Perfectly symmetrical buds develop into broad double blooms, full and fragrant with a characteristic pepper-like

137

scent. The blooms are held in neat clusters on short sturdy stems; indeed all the bloom is at the top of the upright growing plants. This variety remains dominant in its colour range, and in its year of introduction it won the two major awards of the Royal National Rose Society: the President's Trophy and the Clay Vase for perfume.

**Ena Harkness** (34)                    HT
Raised by Norman, Surrey, England
Introduced 1946
*Parentage* Crimson Glory × Southport
Crimson scarlet. The red rose by which all other roses were judged for decades after its introduction. A real shapely blood red that was not too short-petalled or so inclined to turn blue as were most previous crimson hybrid teas. It had an arranging fault in that its neck was never able to support its flower head, which gave the plants a forlorn look. There is some mystery as to its fragrance; some can detect a very distinct perfume, others cannot find a trace. Medium upright habit.

**Ena Harkness** (34)                    C
Climbing form of the bush hybrid tea. A very vigorous climber taking at least two years to become established. Alas the blooms are too heavy for the short flower stems which droop and spoil an otherwise magnificent climber. Height 6–9 m (20–30 ft).

**Ernest H. Morse** (114)            HT
Raised by Kordes, Holstein, Germany
Introduced 1964
*Parentage* unknown
Clear turkey red. Petals are big and ovoid and have a distinct reflex enabling them to give a really good show even in wet weather. Blooms with exceptional fragrance are held sometimes singly, sometimes in clusters, on stout flower stems with strong necks. The rose was named as a tribute to one of the world's great rose hybridists. Vigorous medium height bushes.

**Etude** (216)                            C
Raised by Gregory, Nottingham, England
Introduced 1969
*Parentage* Spectacular × New Dawn
Deep rose pink. A repeat-flowering climber with clusters of twenty to thirty semi-double blooms supported on strong, sturdy laterals. The first summer flush lasts up to eight weeks— thereafter the plant produces a modest succession of flowers until the autumn flush. Trees grow up to 4.5 m (15 ft) tall and do not show a trace of mildew even on draughty walls.

**Europeana** (143)                       F
Raised by de Ruiter, Hazerswoude, Holland
Introduced 1968

138

*Parentage* Ruth Leuwerik × Rosemary Rose
Deepest crimson. Broad camellia-shaped blooms in large well-spaced clusters cover the bush. The red is so deep at times the blooms appear to be black. The foliage is also dark bronze green so it is clearly a rose that can be used to create a dramatic effect. A pleasing feature of the plant is the way the clusters are pulled down almost to the ground by sheer weight of bloom and so clothe the bush most admirably. Inclined to mildew in a bad season.

**Evelyn Fison (174)** F
Raised by McGredy, Auckland, New Zealand
Introduced 1962
*Parentage* Moulin Rouge × Korona
Bright scarlet, almost an iridescent red. A most pleasing characteristic of these blooms is the crinkle look of each petal. This feature hides the stamens almost until the petals are ready to fall, and imparts a neat fresh look to the plants. A really strong plant that will grow and give a fine show almost anywhere. Dark green glossy foliage on neat upright bushes. Vigorous medium height grower.

**Fairy Magic (230)** M
Raised by Moore, California, USA
Introduced 1979
*Parentage* Fairy Moss × unnamed moss seedling
Dark coral pink. Semi-double

blooms formed of ten petals surrounding a large fragrant floret of yellow stamens. A miniature moss rose whose 'mossy' buds are particularly appealing. A taller plant than most miniatures growing in upright fashion to around 45 cm (18 in) tall.

**Fashion (144)** F
Raised by Boerner, New York, USA
Introduced 1949
*Parentage* Pinocchio × Crimson Glory
Soft coral pink. Double blooms, slow to open, are produced freely in large sprays. Petals double over to conceal stamens and help to avoid a 'full blown' look. The flowers have a delicate fragrance to match their soft pastel shades. Historically this rose provided the watershed between the polyanthas and the floribundas. It set a new standard for roses that flowered in clusters, and, having seen what a tremendous impact a double long-lasting rose made upon the public, hybridists and nurserymen immediately turned their attention towards roses that could imitate its style. Medium bushy habit.

**Fashion Flame (279)** M
Raised by Moore, California, USA
Introduced 1977
*Parentage* Little Darling × Fire Princess
Coral orange. Some of the largest buds in proportion to the bush

found in miniature roses. Full double flowers with great petal substance. Long-lasting as a cut bloom. Bushy plants suitable for potting grow to around 30 cm (1 ft) high.

**Fire Princess** (256)    M
Raised by Moore, California, USA
Introduced 1969
*Parentage* Baccara × Eleanor
Brilliant orange-red. The petals of this glowing little miniature are tinged with gold that gives the orange shades an extra brilliance. The colours hold well and deepen rather than fade. A good strong plant producing large flowers for cutting purposes. Useful as a pot plant variety.

**Fleur Cowles** (130)    F
Raised by Gregory, Nottingham, England
Introduced 1972
*Parentage* Queen Elizabeth × Pink Parfait
Cream deepening to buff in the centre petals. Full double blooms, almost hybrid tea size held in clusters, have a pronounced spicy fragrance. Blooms are a favourite of the flower arranger, provide the elegant, 'neat not gaudy' material that forms the basis of a long-lasting masterpiece. Plants are very vigorous upright growers clothed in dark green glossy foliage. Medium to tall grower.

**Fragrant Cloud** (46)    HT
Raised by Tantau, Holstein, Germany
Introduced 1963
*Parentage* unnamed seedling × Prima Ballerina
Also known as Duftwolke. Cinnabar red. Throughout the 1950s and into the 60s rose-growers were looking for a rose that would silence those critics who held that the modern roses had lost their fragrance. Too much emphasis on colour, they contended, had resulted in loss of perfume. This rose complete with both colour and the strongest perfume ever found in a rose was the perfect answer to this challenge. Flowers are produced on healthy bushes against a background of dark green glossy foliage, both singly and in clusters. Vigorous medium habit.

**Fragrant Cloud** (209)    C
A climbing sport of the bush HT. To enjoy this form of the world's most fragrant rose requires patience. The first couple of years give little in the way of flower as all the vigour properly goes into the production of long basal shoots and sturdy laterals. Blooms tend to be produced in clusters of three and are generally somewhat smaller than those found on the bush. The plants are clothed in the usually dark bronze foliage and can be expected to grow up to 6 m (20 ft) or more. Not suitable for north walls.

140

**Fred Loads** (207)                    S

Raised by Holmes, Cheshire, England
Introduced 1968
*Parentage* Dorothy Wheatcroft × Orange Sensation
Bright vermilion. Large open blooms, several to the stem on exceptionally vigorous plants. Perhaps best treated as a tall floribunda and pruned back each year to within 45 cm (18 in) of the base of the plant. This treatment develops a sturdy, self-supporting bush that flowers around the 1.2 m (4 ft) mark and is especially suitable for an informal rose hedge.

**Frensham** (168)                    F

Raised by Norman, Surrey, England
Introduced 1946
*Parentage* unnamed seedling × Crimson Glory
Deep crimson-scarlet. Semi-double blooms held in large trusses. The clusters of bloom are broad and rounded as opposed to having a dominant centre bloom. A vigorous growing bush that survives almost anywhere. Often used as a hedging or border rose because of its impressive flower production and growing performance. Unfortunately there is a weakness in the plant that makes it susceptible to white powdery mildew. An attack can smother the bush in unattractive fungus and ruin its appearance. Tall bushy grower.

**Garden Party** (127)                    HT

Raised by Swim, California, USA
Introduced 1959
*Parentage* Charlotte Armstrong × Peace
Soft creamy yellow flushed with light pink on the edge of the petals. The dominant parent Peace exerts itself in this variety. It would not be inappropriate to describe it as a paler Peace. The size and exquisite form of bloom are almost the same and the bushes are quite vigorous. There is, however, a modest fragrance to be detected in the progeny, all of which attributes add up to a pleasing, delicate rose bloom, that often looks as if it were made from porcelain. Tall vigorous habit.

**Gay Gordons** (96)                    HT

Raised by Cocker, Aberdeen, Scotland
Introduced 1969
*Parentage* Belle Blonde × Karl Herbst
Bright orange and yellow with generous red flushes. Full petalled, long-lasting, well-formed flower. Quite distinct from many other bi-colours which tend to have too harsh a contrast of colours, this bloom is composed of petals gently suffused with gold and orange pigments. An attractive feature of the bush is that it is low-growing and compact, yet very productive of branches and flower. Very good for windy situations. Short bushy habit.

**Gay Maid** (133) F
Raised by Gregory, Nottingham, England
Introduced 1969
*Parentage* Masquerade × Pink Parfait
Saffron yellow base shaded through to carmine. Pointed double buds open slowly into showy full blooms. Many flowers at all stages of development contribute to the cluster. Altogether a happy-looking rose with its tall vigorous habit, masses of light green glossy foliage holding up huge bouquets of colourful bloom. Tall vigorous grower.

**Glenfiddich** (177) F
Raised by Cocker, Aberdeen, Scotland
Introduced 1976
*Parentage* Arthur Bell × (Sabine × Circus)
Deep gold tinted with amber. This variety is often classed as a floribunda HT type as its flowers are akin to the HT, although it flowers in clusters. The brightest golden yellow yet seen in a floribunda. It looks as if it might be rather exotic and delicate until one is reminded that the rose was developed on the windswept hills of northern Aberdeen. The plants grow to medium height, carry their bloom towards the top of the bush and are quite capable of looking after themselves and giving a good show in the most inclement weather. Medium upright habit.

**Gold Coin** (268) M
Raised by Moore, California, USA
Introduced 1967
*Parentage* Golden Glow × Magic Wand
Buttercup yellow. Globular buds and young blooms do not look so attractive as the fully developed flower which curls back on itself to look something like a tiny yellow dahlia. Bushy compact plants growing up to 30 cm (1 ft) tall.

**Golden Angel** (235) M
Raised by Moore, California, USA
Introduced 1975
*Parentage* Golden Glow × (Little Darling × seedling)
Rich butter yellow. Buds like tiny hybrid teas are fragrant and contain an extraordinary number of petals. Useful for cutting and exhibition purposes. A sturdy little plant growing to around 25 cm (10 in) high.

**Golden Giant** (16) HT
Raised by Kordes, Holstein, Germany
Introduced 1961
*Parentage* unknown
Deep golden yellow. Blooms are of the full classic form and generally borne singly on stiff erect stems. As the name suggests the bushes are very vigorous and perhaps a fault is that they are inclined to get leggy and outgrow other roses in the bed. However, the Royal National Rose Society awarded it a Gold Medal for the unfading

142

qualities of the bloom. Tall vigorous grower.

**Golden Sceptre**                    HT
See **Spek's Yellow**

**Golden Showers** (211)          C
Raised by Lammerts, California, USA
Introduced 1956
*Parentage* Charlotte Armstrong × Captain Thomas
Daffodil-yellow. Blooms are small, somewhat untidy in form but very fragrant. Flowers in clusters of three or four blooms. The beauty of this variety lies in the sheer quantity of blooms produced rather than the individual quality of each bloom. The plant grows to around 3 m (10 ft) high and grown against a south-facing wall will give a show of bloom well down towards the base of the plant. The thorns are none too savage and the foliage plentiful, so it is often grown close by doorways where its fragrance can readily be appreciated. An ideal pillar rose.

**Golden Times** (3)              HT
Raised by Cocker, Aberdeen, Scotland
Introduced 1970
*Parentage* Fragrant Cloud × Golden Splendour
Clear lemon yellow. Large well-shaped blooms often as big as 12.5 cm (5 in) across and of exhibition standard. A good quantity of petals (around forty) to ensure good quality flowers without impairing its ability to open without gumming up in a wet season. Sweetly scented for a yellow rose. Sturdy plants with disease-resistant glossy foliage. Medium, branching habit.

**Golden Treasure** (138)         F
Raised by Tantau, Holstein, Germany
Introduced 1964
*Parentage* unknown
Also known as Goldschatz. Strong uncompromising lemon yellow that does not fade away in strong sunlight. A rosette style of bloom that never appears to be fully open. Bushes are tidy, compact growers up to around 60 cm (2 ft) tall. They have a balanced spread and are clothed in medium green glossy foliage. Remains as the best unfading short-growing floribunda since its introduction. Short compact grower.

**Goldgleam** (190)               F
Raised by LeGrice, Norfolk, England
Introduced 1966
*Parentage* Gleaming × Allgold
Clear canary yellow. Full, double and sweetly scented blooms as large as 10 cm (4 in) across. Blooms are held in small tidy clusters on bushes clothed top to bottom in a medium green glossy foliage. Young growth is red and contrasts with the yellow blooms and green leaves. A splendid variety for giving a repeat-flowering performance suitable for mass bedding

143

and extended borders. Medium spreading habit.

**Goldmarie** (183)  F
Raised by Kordes, Holstein, Germany
Introduced 1958
*Parentage* Masquerade × Golden Main
Buds are gold splashed with crimson and open into large golden orange flowers 7.5 and 10 cm (3 and 4 in) across. Extremely fragrant for such a colourful floribunda: A multi-colour variety in which the presence of a good deal of Masquerade blood is evident. Robust bushes, growing on the tall side, bear mid-green healthy glossy foliage and big, sweetly scented, colourful clusters of bloom. Tall shrubby habit.

**Goldschatz**  F
See **Golden Treasure**

**Grandpa Dickson** (102)  HT
Raised by Dickson, Co. Down, N. Ireland
Introduced 1966
*Parentage* (Perfecta × Governador Braga da Cruz) × Piccadilly
Soft clear lemon yellow with a tendency for the tips of the bloom to turn pink in strong sunshine. A pronounced reflex occurs on each petal as it opens beyond the bud stage so that the outer frill of petals looks sharp and pointed. Blooms have high centres and are fit for exhibition purposes. Excellent glossy mid-green foliage; leaves

are slender and look as if they were designed to match the pointed petals. Excellent healthy and vigorous constitution which helped win this variety the coveted President's International Trophy and Gold Medal awarded by the Royal National Rose Society. Vigorous medium habit.

**Green Diamond** (239)  M
Raised by Moore, California, USA
Introduced 1975
*Parentage* unnamed seedling × Sheri Anne
Light green. A tight pink pompon-shaped bud changes to a light green colour as the flower develops. Long-lasting flowers are suitable for exhibition or unusual flower arrangements. The cooler the weather the deeper the shade of green. Strong growing plants to around 30 cm (1 ft) high.

**Gypsy Jewel** (252)  M
Raised by Moore, California, USA
Introduced 1975
*Parentage* Little Darling × Little Buckeroo
Deep coral. Rosette-shaped flowers with a lighter reverse to the tiny pointed petals. Firm, long-lasting blooms, about 3.8 cm (1½ in) across, good for cutting. Healthy plants grow up to around 30 cm (1 ft) tall.

**Hamburg Love** (139)  F
Raised by Timmerman, Nottingham, England
Introduced 1974

*Parentage* Fragrant Cloud × Manx Queen

Rich peach with overtones of deep pink. A pleasing blend of shades rather than contrasting colours form the basis of this most elegant floribunda. Blooms are double and lend themselves to dainty flower arrangements and if cut as young buds will last for several days in water without losing their form. They have the added attraction of being fragrant. Plants do not grow too high and can be useful for planting in front of taller growing varieties to hide their 'legginess'. Short bushy habit.

**Handel** (221)                    C
Raised by McGredy, Auckland, New Zealand
Introduced 1965
*Parentage* Columbine × Heidelberg
Cream edged with a deep rose pink. Petite hybrid tea shaped buds composed of petals, each with a distinctive, but not overpowering, deep pink edge. The habit of flowering in clusters gives the plant a quaint, old-fashioned look. Very free-flowering plants grow to around 3 m (10 ft) high. Good as a pillar rose, on pergolas and fences.

**Happy Thought** (240)            M
Raised by Moore, California, USA
Introduced 1978
*Parentage* (*R. wichuraiana* × Floradora) × Sheri Anne
Warm pink. Fluffy blooms so full

of petals they fold back like pom-pons. Several flowers to the stem and a broad spreading habit suit it for a pot rose or for growing in troughs or rockeries. Plants grow to around 30 cm (1 ft) tall with an 45 cm (18 in) spread.

**Harlow** (118)                    HT
Raised by Cocker, Aberdeen, Scotland
Introduced 1968
*Parentage* Fragrant Cloud × Melrose
Deep salmon pink that blends delightfully with all the pastel shades in roses. Fresh-looking bloom seem to shrug off weather damage, a most important attribute of light-coloured bedding roses. A variety with the proportions and qualities of a successful exhibition rose. Bushes are medium height and exceptionally well clothed in dense, glossy, deep green foliage. Not susceptible to any known rose ailments.

**Harriny** (37)                    HT
Raised by LeGrice, Norfolk, England
Introduced 1967
*Parentage* Pink Favourite × Lively
Delicate shell pink. Extremely large double blooms with high centres are composed of up to forty petals. Perhaps just a shade too many for the uncertain UK climate, as the very delicate colour shows every spot of rain as an unsightly brown blemish.

145

However, you would be hard pressed to find another rose with such exquisite perfume. Bushes are clothed in a contrasting dark green glossy foliage. Flower stems are long and strong. Medium height bushy grower.

**Heart of England** (126)  HT
Raised by Gregory, Nottingham, England
Introduced 1978
*Parentage* Pink Parfait × unnamed seedling
Carmine-rose pink. Strictly speaking this is a floribunda hybrid tea type which means big scented blooms in great profusion. Fine, healthy vigorous bushes make it the ideal bedding rose in the UK, and under its synonym Pink Silk it won the Gold Star of the South Pacific and a Certificate of Merit, as well as the award for the most fragrant hybrid tea in the New Zealand International Rose Awards. Tall vigorous grower.

**Herzog von Windsor**  HT
See **Duke of Windsor**

**Hula Girl** (271)  M
Raised by Williams, Texas, USA
Introduced 1975
*Parentage* Miss Hillcrest × Mabel Dot
Vivid shades of orange. A spectacular flower formed of pointed petals that fill the centre of the bloom so that no stamens are visible. Recommended for cutting or for exhibition. A sturdy, easy-to-grow plant growing up to 30 cm (1 ft) tall.

**Iceberg** (164)  F
Raised by Kordes, Holstein, Germany
Introduced 1958
*Parentage* Robin Hood × Virgo
Also known as Schneewuttchen. Snowy white on a pink base. Really large sprays of sparkling clean blooms. They do take weather damage but there are so many to the bush that the blemishes are not noticed. Bushes are tall and bushy and, if left alone, will grow into shrubs of around 1.5 m (5 ft) tall and have a continuous flowering performance all season long. A pure white highlights all the other colours in the garden. Tall vigorous grower.

**Iceberg** (208)  C
Climbing sport of the bush floribunda. A very vigorous climber up to around 3 m (10 ft). The first flush of bloom is magnificent but the climbing version does not seem to possess a truly recurrent flowering habit, and unlike the bush is devoid of flowers for several weeks during the summer months.

**Iced Ginger** (188)  F
Raised by Dickson, Co. Down, N. Ireland
Introduced 1971
*Parentage* Anne Watkins × unknown

Coppery orange flushed yellow with deep orange veining. Beautifully pointed little buds held in well-spaced fragrant clusters. The most attractive apricot-shaded floribunda yet introduced. The bushes are vigorous once established though they can take a year or two before they send up a good quantity of sturdy branches. Leaves are very dark, glossy and healthy. Medium upright grower.

**Ice White** (197)  F
Raised by McGredy, Auckland, New Zealand
Introduced 1966
*Parentage* Mme Leon Cuny × (Orange Sweetheart × Cinnabar)
Clear brilliant white on a green base. Perhaps even more spectacular than the famous Iceberg. Blooms are like small hybrid tea flowers, each cluster has lots of tight buds with petals that reflex perfectly at the edges. The white floribunda preferred by flower arrangers. Vigorous plants give a generous production of flower sprays with splendidly healthy foliage. Vigorous bushy habit.

**Indian Chief** (112)  HT
Raised by Gregory, Nottingham, England
Introduced 1967
*Parentage* Super Star × unknown
Brilliant currant red shaded through orange to a golden base, almost a bi-colour. High centred blooms with petals that are broad and recurving. Very high quality

blooms produced one at a time on straight, thorny red stems. Alas the foliage is subject to white powdery mildew attack, a condition which mars its appearance during the second half of the season. Vigorous upright grower.

**Invitation** (119)  HT
Raised by Swim and Weeks, California, USA
Introduced 1961
*Parentage* Charlotte Armstrong × Signora
Salmon orange with a yellow base. Long pointed buds, made to look even longer by the sharp reflex of the outer petals, can be as much as 11.5 cm (4½ in) across. One of the most fragrant hybrid teas ever introduced, and although you may not care to have a large bed all of this colour it is worth including a few in every border just for its fragrance. Bushes are rather on the tall side so do not mind blooms being cut as it forms a desirable type of summer pruning. Tall vigorous habit.

**Isabel de Ortiz** (6)  HT
Raised by Kordes, Holstein, Germany
Introduced 1962
*Parentage* unknown
Deep rosy pink with a silvery reverse, a true bi-colour with the novelty appeal. Big fragrant blooms often up to 12.5 cm (5 in) across are very full of petals and are favourites for the exhibition bench. Each bloom has around

forty petals which means that they are very slow to develop and will require to be shielded from the weather if they are destined for the show bench. Very deep bronze foliage. Tall vigorous habit.

**Jamboree** (162)  F
Raised by Gregory, Nottingham, England
Introduced 1964
*Parentage* Masquerade × unknown
A dazzling continuation of cherry red with a clear golden reverse to the petal. Blooms are able to show off their two colours at the same time owing to the unusual globular shape of the blooms which permits both sides of the petal to present their different colour to maximum effect. Big flower sprays and vigorous bushes make this floribunda a real 'show off'. Light green glossy foliage provides a bright cheerful background and completes the effect. Medium bushy habit.

**Janice Tellian** (262)  M
Raised by Moore, California, USA
Introduced 1979
*Parentage* Fair Moss × Fire Princess
Soft rose pink. Dainty yet full blooms formed of many crisp pointed petals, so many of them that they conceal the centres. One of the best pink roses for exhibition work but also good for pots, borders or rockeries. A rounded,

compact, bushy grower, free-flowering and free from disease.

**Jean Rook** (67)  HT
Raised by Gregory, Nottingham, England
Introduced 1978
*Parentage* Grand Gala × unknown
Carmine red with an ivory reverse. The most unusual and striking colour combination ever seen in a hybrid tea rose. This extraordinary rose won the heart of Fleet Street's most controversial journalist whose name it bears. During the trials it was sadly evident that the tidy compact bush was prone to mildew, so both the rose-grower and journalist, though disappointed, retained their integrity and did not release the variety. This rose is included to pay tribute to all the disappointments endured by the hybridist.

**John Waterer** (97)  HT
Raised by McGredy, Auckland, New Zealand
Introduced 1970
*Parentage* King of Hearts × Hanne
Crimson scarlet. Classic high centred blooms with firmly reflexed petals that enable them to open in all weathers. Has all the fragrance one can expect from a deep red rose as well as good strong flower stems to hold the blooms erect. The bushes are strong growers covered in rich dark-green foliage. Named in honour of the founder of the

famous 'Floral Mile' nurseries at Twyford. Medium upright habit.

**Josephine Bruce** (39)  HT
Raised by Bees, Chester, England
Introduced 1949
*Parentage* Crimson Glory ×
Madge Whipp
Dark crimson. Petals have a black velvet-like appearance. Blooms are exactly shaped with tightly curled centres dressed round with fully opened outer petals. They can be as large as 12.5 cm (5 in) across. Often called the 'black' rose, because its colour is so deep. Some people attribute it with a marvellous scent and others deny that the same bloom has any fragrance whatsoever. Bushes are low-growing with a spreading habit, stems are consequently rather short. Low spreading grower.

**Joseph's Coat** (199)  S
Raised by Armstrong & Swim, California, USA
Introduced 1964
*Parentage* Buccaneer × Circus
Red, orange and yellow. A flower that changes colour as it grows. The buds open cardinal red, then change spectacularly to marigold-orange, lemon yellow, crimson and saffron, finishing a fully developed bloom of currant red. Since the flowers are developing at slightly different times it is easy to see how the variety came by its name. The plants can be grown as self-supporting shrub roses or even allowed to grow against a fence as a semi-climber. Prune back to within 45 cm (18 in) of the ground for the first three seasons if a self-supporting shrub is required, thereafter just trim into shape.

**Journey's End** (105)  HT
Raised by Gandy, Rugby, England
Introduced 1978
*Parentage* Doreen × Vienna Charm
Burnt Indian orange, flushed gold. A pronounced reflex gives the outer petals a pointed look whereas the centre of the bloom retains its tightly curled centre. The heavy orange veinage ensures that the bloom looks attractive well into maturity. The bushes are low-growing plants with outward projecting branches, a little untidy, but they do provide good ground cover which helps suppress weed growth.

**Joyce Northfield** (49)  HT
Raised by Northfield, Cambridge, England
Introduced 1977
*Parentage* Fred Gibson × Vienna Charm
Deep apricot. The most elegant of all the pastel-shaded hybrid teas. The blooms are composed of broad, fleshy petals—just enough to give perfect form and not so many as to delay opening until the freshness of the colour has faded away. A clear through colour without contrasting shades to detract from the immaculate form of

149

the bud. It could have just a shade more fragrance but with its vigour and flower production it comes within a hair's breadth of being the perfect rose. Strong upright grower.

**Judy Fischer** (272)    M
Raised by Moore, California, USA
Introduced 1968
*Parentage* Little Darling × Magic Wand
Deep rose pink with soft yellow undertones. An unusual colour combination. Some find it too sombre, but it is difficult to fault the bud or the fully formed bloom. A bushy, compact, trouble-free plant giving a repeat-flowering performance throughout the summer months. Suitable for exhibition work.

**Julia's Rose** (70)    HT
Raised by Tysterman, Wisbech, England
Introduced 1976
*Parentage* Blue Moon × Dr A.J. Verhage
The petals are a subtle blend of parchment and copper tones and often look as if they were made from porcelain. Not just an oddity or novelty but a rare beauty of a rose on plants that give long-stemmed blooms that seem designed for the floral artist after whom it is named. Bushes require a sheltered spot to encourage the production of perfect blooms. (Here is a good greenhouse subject.) Do not prune this variety too hard, as it prefers to grow as big as possible and the cutting of blooms in the summer is usually all it can take. Medium upright habit.

**June Time** (266)    M
Raised by Moore, California, USA
Introduced 1963
*Parentage* (*Rosa wichuraiana* × unnamed seedling
Soft pink. Young buds are cup-shaped; full blooms look just like minute water lilies. Flowers often produced in clusters. Plants have a dark glossy foliage and grow to around 30 cm (1 in) tall.

**Just Joey** (113)    HT
Raised by Cants, Colchester, England
Introduced 1972
*Parentage* Fragrant Cloud × Dr A.J. Verhage
Coppery orange blooms with a distinctive crimp to the outer edge of each very broad petal. Blooms look almost artificial as if they had been made from taffeta. Blooms are as fragrant as one might expect from a rose that has Fragrant Cloud as its parent. A variety that benefits from being planted in a sheltered bed, as the big petals are prone to wind buffeting. Plants are in the medium height range and bear a succession of blooms throughout a long season. Medium, bushy grower.

**Kara** (228)    M
Raised by Moore, California, USA
Introduced 1972

*Parentage* Fairy Moss × Fairy Moss

Pale pink. A single row of no more than six petals form a dainty flower. There is great beauty in the moss that is very prominently displayed on the buds and flower stems. The bushes grow rather taller than regular miniature varieties, as tall as 45 cm (18 in), and have a repeat-flowering habit that tends to compensate for the insignificance of the flower.

**Karl Herbst** (47)                    HT
Raised by Kordes, Holstein, Germany
Introduced 1950
*Parentage* Independence × Peace
Matt scarlet. Very large, beautifully shaped blooms, very many of exhibition quality and very fragrant. The sheer size and quantity of petals (up to sixty) ensured that this variety remained at the top of the Royal National Rose Society's List of Select Roses. In spite of its poor weathering qualities as a garden rose and inclination to turn blue as soon as the bloom reaches maturity it continues to bring success on the show bench. Very vigorous upright habit.

**Kassel** (201)                          S
Raised by Kordes, Holstein, Germany
Introduced 1957
*Parentage* Hamburg × Scarlet Else
Bright cherry-red. Large semi-double blooms in sweetly scented clusters. A plant for a rose border

ideally planted in groups of three plants so that they can nurse each other into 1.5 m (5 ft) high bushes. Prune hard for the first two or three seasons and then just trim the bushes into shape. Recurrent flowering habit.

**Kilworth Gold** (1)                 HT
Raised by Gandy, Rugby, England
Introduced 1977
*Parentage* a sport of Whisky Mac
Golden yellow. Another sport from the prolific Whisky Mac. Tight ovoid buds open to reveal petals with a frilly edge. Blooms are beautifully shaped and fragrant and as with the growing characteristics of the plant are identical to the form of the parent plant. Medium bushy habit.

**King Arthur** (166)                  F
Raised by Harkness, Hertfordshire, England
Introduced 1967
*Parentage* Pink Parfait × Highlight
Salmon pink. Very large, almost hybrid tea sized blooms, so that it is sometimes considered to be a floribunda/hybrid tea type (though its very free-flowering habit tends to favour the floribunda category). Large. Matt medium-green foliage. Medium branching growth around 75 cm ($2\frac{1}{2}$ ft).

**King's Ransom** (28)               HT
Raised by Morey, California, USA
Introduced 1961

*Parentage* Golden Masterpiece ×
Lydia

Clear canary yellow. Tight urn-shaped buds with petals that curl outwards at their tips ensure that the bloom never gums up in wet weather. In 1961 it was hailed as the 'breakthrough' in yellow roses, as it embodied these desirable qualities. It did not fade, its blooms retained their youthful bud shape for a long time and the bushes were not so tall and leggy as its predecessors. It was awarded the All American Championship and many other great rose trophies in recognition of these several desirable characteristics. Medium upright habit.

**Köln am Rhein** (205)          s

Raised by Kordes, Holstein, Germany

Introduced 1956

*Parentage* unknown

Also known as Cologne. Deep salmon pink with a lighter centre. The blooms look their best when fully open when their semi-double form looks delightfully 'old fashioned'. The bushes are clothed in a wealth of glossy dark green foliage. A repeat-flowering habit on plants that grow up to 1.5 m (5 ft) high.

**Korona** (194)          F

Raised by Kordes, Holstein, Germany

Introduced 1955

*Parentage* unknown

Orange scarlet. Two rows of petals form a most colourful eye-catching bloom further enhanced by bright golden stamens as the petals unfurl. Unusually large blooms (up to 6.3 cm, $2\frac{1}{2}$ in) are produced continually on larger than usual bushes. Almost a shrub rose in style of growth so it can easily be employed as a hedging variety or as a tall informal border rose. Tall bushy habit.

**Lady Belper** (60)          HT

Raised by Verschuren, Haps, Holland

Introduced 1948

*Parentage* Mrs G.A. van Rossem × unnamed seedling

Apricot shaded orange-bronze. Large semi-globular blooms are full of fragrance. An unusual colour in its year of introduction paving the way for the hard to come by apricot-coloured hybrid teas. Most roses in this shade were to be regarded with suspicion as they tended to be prone to mildew attack but this variety had dark bronze stems and deep glossy foliage that resisted the disease. Medium bushy grower.

**Lady Grade** (95)          HT

Raised by Gregory, Nottingham, England

Introduced 1982

*Parentage* Summer Holiday × unknown

Soft orange vermilion. Blooms often up to 12.5 cm (5 in) across when open are held individually and several to the stem. Long pointed buds develop into high centred blooms ideal for bedding or cutting purposes. Flower arrangers love its crisp clear colour which, though vibrant, is not overpoweringly dominant. Bushes are healthy and vigorous and flourish in the medium height category.

**Lady of the Sky (124)** HT
Raised by Gregory, Nottingham, England
Introduced 1974
*Parentage* Queen Elizabeth × Summer Holiday
Clear geranium lake. Strictly speaking this is yet another example of the floribunda hybrid tea type of rose. The buds resemble dainty hybrid tea shaped flowers which develop always several to the stem. This clear coral rose is an ideal trouble-free bedding variety but it is also grown for the masses of cut blooms it regularly produces. A Queen Elizabeth seedling that inherits a lot of the vigour and disease-resistance of its parent. Tall upright habit.

**Lady Sylvia (21)** HT
Raised by Stevens, Hertfordshire, England
Introduced 1926
*Parentage* a sport of Madame Butterfly
Soft blush pink suffused with apricot. Long elegant buds of a colour that could so easily be called 'bridal pink' are always in demand by the florist who loves to use them in wedding bouquets and bridesmaids' posies. Bushes will grow very tall if allowed and are best treated to a light pruning. Tall bushy grower.

**Lady Sylvia (21)** C
Climbing sport of the bush hybrid tea, which itself is a sport of the hybrid tea Madame Butterfly. A very vigorous plant that can be expected to grow up to 6 m (20 ft) or more. Pruning this variety will result in the loss of blooms following season as the inclination of the plant is to replace growth before flowering. The climbing form seems to be particularly sweetly scented, perhaps for no reason other than that there is such a large concentration of flowers together on the plant at one time.

**Lancastrian (128)** HT
Raised by Gregory, Nottingham, England
Introduced 1965
*Parentage* Ena Harkness × unknown
Rich crimson. Beautiful spiral-shaped buds, often described as an improved Ena Harkness. It has good colour that does not turn blue when cut, good perfume, which is sometimes hard to find in Ena Harkness, and good strong necks that enable the blooms to stand erect in the vase. Trees are very thorny and full of dark green glossy foliage that is free from mildew. Tall vigorous habit.

153

**Landora** HT
See **Sunblest**

**Lavender Jewel** (231) M
Raised by Moore, California, USA
Introduced 1978
*Parentage* Little Chief × Angel
Face
Lavender-mauve. Deepest of the
lavender miniatures with well-
shaped buds that are very good as
cut blooms. The colour does not
fade and the flowers are very slow
to open. Plants grow to around 30
cm (1 ft), are compact neat growers
with dark green foliage.

**Lavender Lace** (234) M
Raised by Moore, California, USA
Introduced 1968
*Parentage* Ellen Poulsen × Debbie
Soft lavender. Fragrant, shapely
buds. Free-flowering plants with a
bushy compact habit useful for a
rockery. A useful colour to in-
corporate into a 'blue' garden
scheme.

**Lavender Lassie** (202) S
Raised by Kordes, Holstein,
Germany
Introduced 1960
*Parentage* unknown
Lavender pink. Very full blooms
up to 7.5 cm (3 in) across held in
clusters. A hybrid musk rose with
a pronounced fragrance. Bushes
grow as high as 1.5 m (5 ft) tall
with a repeat-flowering habit.
Plants tend to become top heavy
with tall shoots and big clusters of
bloom and require to be pruned

hard back for the first three years
after planting. This ensures that
the bush has a broad base on
which to support subsequent
shrub-like growth.

**Lavender Princess** (195) F
Raised by Boerner, New York
State, USA
Introduced 1959
*Parentage* World's Fair seedling ×
Lavender Pinocchio
Lavender flushed lilac pink. A
peculiar form of semi-double
bloom that leaves the innermost
petals nestling around and con-
cealing the stamens while the
outer petals open out flat to produce flowers that are around 7.5
cm (3 in) across. Moderately fragrant flowers are held at the top of
sturdy branching bushes. Vigorous upright habit.

**Lemon Delight** (233) M
Raised by Moore, California, USA
Introduced 1978
*Parentage* Fairy Moss × Gold
Moss
Lemon yellow. Long pointed
mossy buds opens into a dainty
ten-petalled yellow flower with a
charming lemon-like fragrance. A
miniaturised moss rose that grows
rather more vigorously than most
miniatures and can be expected to
obtain a height of around 45 cm
(1½ ft).

**Leslie G. Harris** (104) HT
Raised by Gregory, Nottingham,
England

Introduced 1970
*Parentage* Super Star × Josephine Bruce
Crimson red. Full shapely blooms with acutely reflexing velvet-like petals that shrug off rain damage. Very strong stems that do not allow the flowers to droop. Robust, healthy bushes do not grow much over 60 cm (2 ft) tall and as a consequence are always among the first varieties to bloom each season. Useful as a cut rose or a dwarf bedding variety. Short upright habit.

**Leslie Johns** (72)                HT
Raised by Gregory, Nottingham, England
Introduced 1972
*Parentage* Soraya × unnamed seedling
Rose Bengal. Full conical blooms often reaching exhibition standard without special attention. High pointed blooms are formed of rather soft fleshy petals that do need protection from the rain to be certain of blemish-free specimens. An exhibitor's rose in size, style and quality, but not quite so successful as a general garden variety. Tall bushy trees clothed in dark green foliage.

**Lilli Marlene** (192)                F
Raised by Kordes, Holstein, Germany
Introduced 1959
*Parentage* Our Princess × Rudolph Timm
Deep velvety red. Long-lasting double blooms held towards the top of very generous bushes. One of the favoured varieties for the massed bedding effect achieved by local authorities in parks and public gardens in Europe. Tough leathery foliage that defies mildew attack. A wonderfully generous plant that seems to be able to look after itself. Medium bushy habit.

**Lily de Gerlache** (45)                HT
Raised by Experimental Station, Melle, Belgium
Introduced 1971
*Parentage* Perfecta × Prima Ballerina
Cherry pink flushed gold. High pointed buds hold their centres until the blooms have developed to perfection. A real exhibitor's rose, cup-shaped and full of fragrance. The winner of the Henry Edland Memorial Medal for being the most fragrant rose on trial during the year of its introduction into the UK. As with most exhibition roses, it marks badly in wet weather and blooms destined for the exhibition bench need careful protection. Trees are very healthy and productive. Vigorous, bushy grower.

**Little Flirt** (258)                M
Raised by Moore, California, USA
Introduced 1961
*Parentage* (*Rosa wichuraiana* × Floradora) × (Golden Glow × Zee)
Orange red with a yellow reverse. Rather large petals form a colour-

155

ful though untidy bloom. One of the largest miniatures that might have to be 'tamed' with the secateurs every other season if it is not to outgrow its welcome. The colours tend to fade as the blooms mature.

**Living Fire (148)**            F
Raised by Gregory, Nottingham, England
Introduced 1972
*Parentage* Super Star × unnamed seedling
A blend of gold orange and flame red, never was a rose more aptly named. Full blooms, slow to open, eventually demonstrate an unusual characteristic in that the centre petals turn the flower into a pompon type of rose. The stamens remain concealed until the petals shatter and prevent the mature blooms from looking full blown and tired. Bushes are willing growers and produce most of their flower clusters towards the top of the plant. Medium upright habit.

**Lord Louis (94)**            HT
Raised by Gregory, Nottingham, England
Introduced 1982
*Parentage* Pink Favourite × unnamed seedling
Deep velvet red. Long urn-shaped buds with neatly furled petals compose one of the world's most elegant red roses. Long strong flower stems dressed in the glossiest deep green foliage ever seen on a rose provide a perfect foil for each bloom. Flowers are held singly to the stem so suit the variety for cutting purposes although the flawless foliage demands to be shown off as a background to a massed bedding rose. Medium upright habit.

**Lovers' Meeting (9)**            HT
Raised by Gandy, Rugby, England
Introduced 1980
*Parentage* Egyptian Treasure × unnamed seedling
Orange vermilion. It is most unusual for a new colour break to occur in roses, but in 1980, just when the rose growers were thinking that there was nothing new, along came yet another distinct shade, a colour that attracts the eye and demands attention.This rose has neat and tidy buds that develop into showy shapely blooms. The petals fall before the colour fades and so gives the tall, vigorous bushes a tidy appearance. Foliage is medium green, clean and healthy. Medium to tall upright habit.

**Love Token (134)**            F
Raised by Gregory, Nottingham, England
Introduced 1964
*Parentage* unknown
Soft rose pink. A most unusual form of bloom in that each petal is crimped as well as having heavily scalloped edges so that the flower, when fully opened, is attractively flat and full. Blooms of this type are produced in big well spaced

clusters on healthy bushes that send up a good supply of fresh basal shoots to replace spent flower spray. Medium upright habit.

**Madame Henri Guillot** (24)  HT
Raised by Mallerin, Isere, France
Introduced 1938
*Parentage* Rochefort × unnamed seedling
Orange pink and red. Truly conical-shaped buds are the distinctive feature of this bloom which contains only twenty-five petals and as a consequence is not subject to weather damage. This was the first real break from the very heavily petalled hybrid teas that were so unsuited to the wet UK summers and often had to have their outside petals peeled before they would open. Medium height bushy grower.

**Madame Henri Guillot** (24)  C
A climbing sport of the bush HT. Particularly attractive as a climber as the plant is clothed in broad and glossy green foliage. Grows up to 6 m (20 ft) high, and suitable for a house wall. A vigorous plant that tends to grow leggy and bare at the base if the basal shoots are not grown horizontally, thus permitting the lateral growth to provide coverage.

**Magic Carousel** (245)  M
Raised by Moore, California, USA
Introduced 1972

*Parentage* Little Darling ×
Westmont
White with a red outer edge to each petal. Full, long-lasting blooms look their best when fully open. A novel confection of colours that is guaranteed to catch the judge's eye and serve it well as an exhibition variety. Neat and tidy plants grow to around 25 cm (10 in) tall.

**Mainzer Fastnacht**  HT
See **Blue Moon**

**Manx Queen** (155)  F
Raised by A. Dickson, Co. Down, N. Ireland
Introduced 1963
*Parentage* Shepherd's Delight ×
Circus
Gold and red. The young buds first show colour as deep bronze-red, but soon display rich golden yellow petals flushed with pink. Blooms are held three or more to the stem and owe their beauty to their generous display of colour rather than shapeliness. They are vigorous, bushy growers.

**Ma Perkins** (170)  F
Raised by Boerner, New York State, USA
Introduced 1952
*Parentage* Red Radiance ×
Fashion
Pearly pink. Cup-shaped double blooms in large clusters. It is difficult to imagine the impact such double floribundas made on the rose world during the 1950s. Most

cluster roses were single or at the most semi-double, and these new double varieties were instantly recognised as being an improved strain. The Americans contributed Fashion and then this variety to set new standards for floribundas, roses so different from what went before they that coined a new name for the type. Medium bushy growing plant.

**Margaret Merril** (182)    F
Raised by Harkness, Hertfordshire, England
Introduced 1977
*Parentage* Rudolph Timm × (Dedication × Pascali)
Pure white. Pretty, delicate-looking buds have just enough petals to fill out cup-shaped dainty yet large (up to 10 cm, 4 in) open blooms. The most outstandingly fragrant rose many gardeners will ever experience. The white flowers are overlaid with a sheen of satin pink, and although they are petite in the bud they combine the charm of both old-fashioned and modern roses. Best grown as a medium height variety. Vigorous bushy habit.

**Maria** (198)    F
Raised by Gregory, Nottingham, England
Introduced 1965
*Parentage* unnamed seedling × Border King
Strawberry red. Only a single row of ten petals but each is heavily flounced at the edges which makes

the broad blooms look most attractive. The clusters of blooms are extra large and since each of the flowers is up to 7.5 cm (3 in) across each stem can provide a bouquet of flowers. The foliage of this variety is amongst the broadest ever seen and is clean and disease-free. Unfortunately this lovely rose was introduced just as the single polyantha roses were going out of fashion and although it was undisputably one of the most beautiful of its type it did not fall in with the popular demand which was for double blooms.

**Marlena** (152)    F
Raised by Kordes, Holstein, Germany
Introduced 1964
*Parentage* Gertrud Westphal × Lilli Marlene
Deep crimson. Semi-double blooms, two rows of ruffled petals in clusters of five or six blooms. The bushes are on the short side, neat and tidy growers up to around 45 cm (18 in) high. A very good variety for growing against low retaining walls, picture windows or ponds. A repeat-flowering variety all season long. Short compact grower.

**Mary Marshall** (251)    M
Raised by Moore, California, USA
Introduced 1970
*Parentage* Little Darling × Fairy Princess
Orange with a yellow reverse. A rather loose large flower that tends

to lose its shape when fully open. Plants grow on the tall side, around 38 cm (15 in), and with flowers up to 3.8 cm (1½ in) across they can look like a small flowering shrub.

**Masquerade** (137)                F
Raised by Boerner, New York State, USA
Introduced 1949
*Parentage* Goldilocks × Holiday
Buds open yellow, turn salmon pink and eventually deep red. Semi-double blooms at all stages of development on exceptionally large clusters make for the most colourful rose ever. The bushes grow to be as tall as 1.2 m (4 ft) high without support and never fail to produce a magnificent show, the more sunshine the deeper the red pigmentation in the mature blooms and the wider the contrast of colours. A disappointing feature of the variety is that when the first flush of bloom is over there is no replacement flower until the autumn. Nevertheless there will never be a happier rose to grace a garden. Tall bushy grower.

**Masquerade** (218)                C
A climbing sport of the bush floribunda. Most spectacular is its spring flush of bloom but thereafter the plant is rather uninteresting, except for the amount of seed pods the plant sustains. Tends to grow rather 'leggy' leaving the first 1–1.2 m (3–4 ft) of the stems bare of flower or foliage.

**Matangi** (167)                F
Raised by McGredy, Auckland, New Zealand
Introduced 1974
*Parentage* unnamed seedling × Picasso
Deep orange shaded yellow. A double bloom composed of three rows of colourful petals, the reverse side a bright contrast to the face. A development of what were aptly named the handpainted roses, since each bloom resembled but was slightly different from its neighbour in the same cluster. This rose is representative of a whole range of floribundas ranging from the novel Picasso to the dainty Sue Lawley. Medium height bushy grower.

**Mayflower** (18)                HT
Raised by Gregory, Nottingham, England
Introduced 1958
*Parentage* Eden Rose × unknown
Carmine with a silver reverse. A most unusual bi-colour. An exciting bedding variety with a delightfully pronounced fragrance. Most of the extraordinary bi-colour combinations did not prove as popular as their originators had expected, and their catalogue life was relatively short. Deep green glossy foliaged plants in the medium height range.

**McGredy's Sunset** (13)  HT
Raised by McGredy, Belfast, N. Ireland
Introduced 1936
*Parentage* Margaret McGredy × Mabel Morse
Yellow shading to orange on the face of the petal, the reverse a clear buttercup yellow. In its year of introduction this was the most brilliant hybrid tea, the first of the bi-colours. Though not to be compared with the twin-coloured varieties that were to follow, it pointed towards a new direction for the hybridist to follow. It was decades, however, before the beautiful fragrance of this rose was restored to the bi-colours. Tall vigorous grower.

**McGredy's Yellow** (93)  HT
Raised by McGredy, Belfast, N. Ireland
Introduced 1933
*Parentage* Mrs Charles Lamplough × (Queen Alexandra × J.B. Clark)
Soft lemon yellow. Long bud formed of cup-shaped petals. When introduced this variety was considered to be the supreme yellow rose and capable of resisting weather damage. By modern standards it has poor weathering characteristics and is sparsely clothed with meagre foliage. The premier yellow garden rose for many decades only to be reconsidered after the post war introduction of Spek's Yellow and Buccaneer. Medium upright grower.

**Message** (99)  HT
Raised by Meilland, Cap d'Antibes, France
Introduced 1955
*Parentage* Virgo × Peace
Also known as White Knight. Clear white with a hint of green at the base of the petal. A full shapely bloom with gently reflexing petals. As with most white roses it is inclined to suffer rain damage. The greenish base is desirable for flower arrangers looking for a white rose without a trace of pink. Foliage is on the small side, is matt green and inclined to mildew in a bad season. Medium height grower.

**Mildred Scheel**  HT
See **Deep Secret**

**Mischief** (4)  HT
Raised by McGredy, Auckland, New Zealand
Introduced 1961
*Parentage* Peace × Spartan
Coral salmon. Tiny buds first start to show colour when they are the size of the tip of your little finger, yet develop into big broad exquisitely-shaped fragrant blooms. Left alone the blooms grow in clusters and provide a mass of colour. Disbudded they provide cutting roses that can often reach exhibition quality. The winner of the RNRS President's Trophy with high points for fragrance and vigorous disease-free growth. Medium bushy habit.

**Mister Lincoln** (42)  HT
Raised by Swim and Weeks, California, USA
Introduced 1964
*Parentage* Chrysler Imperial × Charles Mallerin
Rich dark crimson. Inner heart of the bloom is a slightly lighter shade than the almost black velvet-like petals that fold back to form one of the most attractive red roses ever grown. The blooms yield the sweet fragrance one might well expect from a deep red rose and do not disappoint by displaying weather damage or mildew blemishes. Dark foliage with bronze new growth show off a magnificent red rose. Tall vigorous grower.

**Mojave** (41)  HT
Raised by Swim, California, USA
Introduced 1954
*Parentage* Charlotte Armstrong × Signora
Burnt orange with deeper orange veining. Strikingly decorative buds that are long and cylindrical with only the outer most petals showing any inclination to reflex back and allow the centres to develop. As a consequence of the long stems in association with these tight lasting buds it has become a favourite cutting variety. Medium upright habit, bright glossy foliage.

**Monique** (14)  HT
Raised by Meilland, Cap d'Antibes, France

Introduced 1949
*Parentage* Lady Sylvia × unnamed seedling
Soft pink flushed salmon pink. A cup-shaped bloom consisting of broad petals that look as if they were made of a silken material. Sweetly scented blooms on short stems are produced all over the bush. Up to the introduction of this variety many pink roses tended to produce deformed blooms in the early summer and this was the first rose introduced after the Second World War to correct this disorder and challenge the prominence of Lady Sylvia and Madame Butterfly. Medium height bushy plants.

**Montezuma** (86)  H
Raised by Swim, California, USA
Introduced 1955
*Parentage* Fandango × Floradora
Buds tinted red, full blooms salmon red. High centred blooms produced in big clusters. When disbudded the vigour of the stem is poured into the centre bloom to produce flowers of exhibition quality. In the warm summer zone of the USA that can guarantee a week free from rain the blooms can develop to perfection. In the UK the quality of bloom is easily obtained but it must be shielded from wind and precipitation. The inclination of the full bloom to 'blue' with age often gives away the fact that the bloom has been 'held back' a day or so past its

161

prime. Vigorous tall upright grower.

**Mood Music** (232)                M
Raised by Moore, California, USA
Introduced 1977
*Parentage* Fairy Moss × Gold Moss
Orange shaded to peachy pink. A miniaturised moss rose that produces spectacularly large double blooms on plants that grow up to around 45 cm (18 in) tall. The mossy appearance of the buds is created by soft thin thorns that grow the length of the stem to the tips of the sepals. Flowers are long-lasting, make for good cut blooms but do tend to fade in strong sunlight.

**Mrs Sam McGredy** (26)        HT
Raised by McGredy, Belfast, N. Ireland
Introduced 1929
*Parentage* (Donald McDonald × Golden Emblem) × (seedling × Queen Alexandra)
Coppery-orange red. The essence of the modern garden rose is embodied in the handsome form of this rose introduced in 1929. For a generation it remained, along with Crimson Glory and Lady Sylvia, one of the most popular garden roses. By modern standards it had little vigour and latterly the climbing sport of the variety was recommended rather than the bush. The foliage is deepest bronze a perfect foil for the blooms. Medium spreading habit.

**Mrs Sam McGredy** (26)          C
A climbing sport of the bush hybrid tea. One of the most popular coppery-orange climbers since its discovery on several nurseries around 1940. Growth is limited to about 3 m (10 ft), so its best application is as a pillar or pergola rose. Sad to say the climbing form is similar to the bush in showing little resistance to black spot disease.

**Mullard Jubilee** (106)        HT
Raised by McGredy, Auckland, New Zealand
Introduced 1970
*Parentage* Paddy McGredy × Prima Ballerina
Also known as Electron. Deep rose-pink. Shapely buds on the strongest, thickest, thorniest rose stems ever seen on a hybrid tea rose. The parentage gives a clue to its attributes, the abundant flower production emanating from Paddy McGredy and the vigour of the plant coming from Prima Ballerina. The blooms are possessed of a beautiful fragrance and unusually long life. A true bedding rose. Medium sturdy grower.

**My Choice** (35)               HT
Raised by LeGrice, Norfolk, England
Introduced 1958
*Parentage* Wellworth × Ena Harkness
Carmine pink on the upper face of the petal with a pale yellow reverse. A plum-shaped bloom, the

outer petals flare away from the base and the centre is held to a tight point. An attractive bicolour with exceptional fragrance, and a trouble-free constitution. Winner of the RNRS Clay Challenge Trophy for its perfume and a Gold Medal for its performance on the Trials Ground. Often shown to perfection as an exhibition rose. Vigorous upright trouble-free habit.

**My Girl** (175)                    F
Raised by de Ruiter, Hazerswoude, Holland
Introduced 1964
*Parentage* Decapo × unnamed seedling
Deep salmon. Buds resemble the flowers of the camellia. They are sweetly scented, maintain quite dainty proportions and bloom in large clusters. There is a tendency for the sprays to droop slightly under the sheer weight of bloom they have to carry. The bushes are healthy but a shade untidy for a formal garden setting. This, together with its unusual look, are the reasons for it not becoming established as a favourite variety. Medium bushy habit.

**My Valentine** (257)                    M
Raised by Moore, California, USA
Introduced 1975
*Parentage* Little Chief × Little Curt
Crimson. Full double flowers 2.5 cm (1 in) across when open contain as many as sixty small petals that

ensure the heart of the bloom remains concealed even when they are fully opened. A bushy well-foliaged plant that grows vigorously 25–35 cm (10–14 in) high. Shows a good resistance to mildew, a weakness seen in a lot of red miniatures.

**New Penny** (261)                    M
Raised by Moore, California, USA
Introduced 1962
*Parentage* (*Rosa wichuraiana* × Floradora) × unnamed seedling
Orange red buds, coral pink flowers. Blooms have relatively few pointed petals that soon open to reveal the flower's prominent yellow stamens. A reasonably pronounced fragrance can be detected. Bushy plants with broad glossy, dark green foliage grow to around 25 cm (10 in).

**News** (140)                    F
Raised by Le Grice, Norfolk, England
Introduced 1968
*Parentage* Lilac Charm × Tuscany Superb
Purple red. Perhaps the least significant characteristic of this rose is the semi-single form of the petal which is composed of no more than ten broad petals spaced round a cluster of bright yellow stamens. The real impact is created by the vivid uncompromising purple colour and the sheer mass of bloom carried by the plant. A variety that solicits an immediate response of like or dislike and that

requires careful thought when planning a colour scheme. Medium height, free-branching grower.

**Nozomi** (280) CM
Raised by Onodera, Tokyo, Japan
Introduced 1968
*Parentage* Fairy Princess × Sweet Fairy
Pearl pink. A single row of petals makes for a rather insignificant little flower but there are so many to each long branch that the plant takes on a simple beauty. Prostrate-growing plants that produce fronds up to 1 m (3 ft) long that have a habit of flowering on the previous year's wood. The plants will climb, tumble over retaining walls, cover banks and grow on patios. Flower production is intense for around two months; thereafter only a few blooms are produced. A good ground cover plant with tiny cotoneaster-like leaves.

**Orangeade** (135) F
Raised by McGredy, Auckland, New Zealand
Introduced 1964
*Parentage* Orange Sweetheart × Independence
Bright vermilion orange. A semi-double bloom most beautiful when fully open to reveal the contrasting golden yellow stamens. A very vigorous bush that produces flower continuously throughout the summer. Its introduction coincided with the advent of the long lasting 'double' floribundas and it did not enjoy the popularity that such a beautiful and vigorous rose might have expected. One of the most eye-catching and trouble-free bedding floribundas ever introduced. Vigorous branching habit.

**Orange Honey** (246) M
Raised by Moore, California, USA
Introduced 1979
*Parentage* Rumba × Over the Rainbow
Orange and yellow. The centre petals are a deep golden yellow, but the edges of the outermost row are tinged with pink. Just like Masquerade the colours deepen the more sunshine they experience. The blooms are surprisingly fragrant for a miniature rose. Repeat-flowering, like a small floribunda, growing up to around 30 cm (1 ft) high. The brightest and most vibrant of all the miniature roses.

**Orange Sensation** (159) F
Raised by de Ruiter, Hazerswoude, Holland
Introduced 1961
*Parentage* unknown
Orange flame. At the time of its introduction a bright new colour in floribundas. Double blooms consisting of more than twenty petals, held in big bunches on plants that conform nicely to the requirements of a formal rose garden. Tidy plants flowering at around 75 cm ($2\frac{1}{2}$ ft) high. The

blooms have an unusual fragrance, just like that of a Cox's Orange Pippin apple. During its first year of introduction it was awarded a Gold Medal by the Royal National Rose Society and two Gold Medals by the Floriade Rotterdam, as well as numerous Certificates of Merit, all serving to demonstrate its significance in the world of roses in 1961. Medium height upright grower.

**Orange Silk** (173)    F
Raised by McGredy, Auckland, New Zealand
Introduced 1968
*Parentage* Orangeade  ×  (Ma Perkins × Independence)
Orange vermilion. Buds resemble the shape of young hybrid tea flowers, dainty and elegant, then open to form part of a neat colourful cluster. This variety might well be described as an improved Orange Sensation. It is altogether a neater and more compact grower and produces more bloom for its size than the former. The plants can be maintained at around 45 cm (18 in) high which fits them for planting against low retaining walls, at the base of picture windows or alongside narrow paths. The blooms have a sweet, apple-like fragrance. Short compact habit.

**Over the Rainbow** (244)    M
Raised by Moore, California, USA
Introduced 1972

*Parentage* Little   Darling   × Westmont
Red and yellow bi-colour. Buds are high centred, like small hybrid tea blooms, in fact just like a miniature 'Piccadilly'. A very shapely show rose that can be exhibited to perfection if the developing blooms are sheltered from the worst of the weather. Plants grow vigorously to around 30 cm (12 in) high, bushy and well foliaged, a good variety for potting.

**Paddy McGredy** (179)    F
Raised by McGredy, Auckland, New Zealand
Introduced 1962
*Parentage* Spartan × Tzigane
Deepest rose pink. Blooms take on the form of small hybrid tea buds and literally smother the bush leaving little room for foliage. The most floriferous of all the floribundas. The bushes are low-growing and are easily maintained at around 45–60 cm (1½–2 ft). The flowers are bunched so tightly on the bush that the spent blooms need to be removed from time to time. A gentle shake of the bush is all that is required to remove the unsightly brown petals and the bush looks full and fresh again. Disease-free,   short   compact grower.

**Pamela's Choice** (44)    HT
Raised by Bardill, Nottingham, England
Introduced 1966

165

*Parentage* a sport of Piccadilly
Deep golden yellow. A moderately
full bloom of medium size opens
rather quickly and spoils its bud
shape. This is a 'sport' from the
colourful bi-colour 'Piccadilly'
and the plants resemble the parent
in every respect and possess
abundant coppery green foliage
highly resistant to disease. Vigorous bushy upright grower.

**Panorama Holiday** (91)     HT
Raised by Gregory, Nottingham,
England
Introduced 1973
*Parentage* Queen Elizabeth × unnamed seedling
Peach pink shading to dawn pink.
Sweetly scented buds held in
Queen Elizabeth type clusters.
After the centre bud has developed the subsidiary buds all
bloom at the same time and provide a magnificent display. The
colour is much softer than rose
pink and does not fade away to an
unsightly white when the bloom is
fully matured. A very strong
disease-free bush with dark broad
glossy foliage to dress the base of
the plant whilst the bloom seems
to prefer to grow in a mass at the
top of the plant. The perfect bedding rose. Tall vigorous habit.

**Papa Meilland** (31)        HT
Raised by Meilland, Cap
d'Antibes, France
Introduced 1963

*Parentage* Chrysler Imperial  ×
Charles Mallerin
Darkest crimson outer petals,
almost black, contrasting with a
lighter crimson centre. Petals are
often described as velvet-like,
none more so than these of what is
often called the 'black rose'. The
shape of the blooms can be described as the perfect rose shape
with the reflexing petals furled
round a high centre. There are a
couple of disappointing characteristics which could deter one from
laying down a bed of this variety.
One is its inclination to mildew in
the UK and the second is that it is
rather shy. Medium upright habit.

**Paprika** (158)              F
Raised by Tantau, Holstein,
Germany
Introduced 1958
*Parentage* Marchenland  ×  Red
Favourite
Glowing orange red with a bluish
tinge at the base of each petal. A
bloom that is at its most decorative
when fully open. One of the most
attractive and decorative semi-
double floribundas ever introduced. Unfortunately the vogue
for double floribundas was at its
height at the time of its introduction and it did not receive the
attention it deserved. A sad victim
of commercial considerations that
remains as one of the most beautiful bedding roses of all time.
Medium bushy habit.

**Paris Match** (77)   HT
Raised by Meilland, Cap d'Antibes, France
Introduced 1957
*Parentage* Independence × Grandmère Jenny
Carmine to rose pink. Ovoid-shaped blooms composed of broad flat petals. The high pointed tight centre is just what the exhibitor desires in a rose, and the wide spread of the outer petals gives the bloom a 'quality' look. The fleshy petals have little weather resistance and need to be shielded from rain and wind. Plants have broad leathery textured foliage with good disease resistance. Medium bushy grower.

**Pascali** (122)   HT
Raised by Lens, Wauve-Notre-Dame, Belgium
Introduced 1963
*Parentage* Queen Elizabeth × White Butterfly
White with a cream base. A moderately full bloom with just enough petals (thirty) to impart form without retarding the initial opening of the bud. White roses are all prone to weather damage though it is generally accepted that this variety has the best resistance to rain spotting and 'gumming up' of any of the current varieties and is the only white hybrid tea that could be considered for bedding work. It also has good resistance to mildew, which is another weakness in this class of rose. Tall and bushy habit.

**Peace** (81)   HT
Raised by Meilland, Cap d'Antibes, France
Introduced 1945
*Parentage* (George Dickson × Souvenir de Claudius Pernet) × (Joanna Hill × Charles P. Kilham)
Golden yellow edged pink. Immaculately-formed blooms commence as mostly yellow buds with a tinge of pink on the edge of the petals. As the flower develops so the pink pigmentation increases, a feature that not only disguises any fading but adds to its beauty. The growth foliage and flower production of the bushes is without equal. Broad glossy leaves ward off disease and contribute a charming background to the huge colourful blooms. The most famous hybrid tea of all time, and the rose by which all other roses are judged. Tall vigorously bushy habit.

**Peace** (81)   C
A climbing sport of the bush hybrid tea. Something of a disaster for growers who cannot afford to wait the years it almost always requires to become established. A huge plant that eventually looks magnificent, although pruning will further delay blooming until the growth has made up. With this sort of reputation it is nowadays seldom offered for sale.

**Peachy White** (236)   M
Raised by Moore, California,USA
Introduced 1976

*Parentage* Little Darling × Red Germain

Near white buds showing a tinge of pink as they develop. The whitest of the white miniatures with a lovely bud shape, though it is disappointing to see the blooms 'blow' open so quickly but this is the consequence of there being only eighteen petals in each flower. Plants are vigorous with long flower stems growing to a height of around 30 cm (1 ft).

**Pebble Mill** (20)  HT

Raised by Gregory, Nottingham, England

Introduced 1973

*Parentage* Paddy McGredy × unnamed seedling

Silver centre surrounded by magenta. A novelty rose that looks its best at the mid-point of its opening sequence. The inner petals do have a surprising silvery appearance that contrasts with the spiraea-red outer petals. Not everyone's preference, but it certainly looks different. Unlike many novelty types this variety is unaffected by bad weather, and has good repeat-flowering qualities. So many blooms to the stem it might reasonably be classed as a large-flowered floribunda. Medium bushy habit.

**Percy Thrower** (48)  HT

Raised by Lens, Wauve-Notre-Dame, Belgium

Introduced 1964

*Parentage* La Jolla × Karl Herbst

Silvery rose pink. Blooms formed of crisp pink petals that open slowly into flattish broad blooms with a low pointed centre. The clearest pink of all the hybrid teas with excellent weathering characteristics—a real flower arranger's rose. Its one drawback is its low spreading habit which does not very well conform to formal planting arrangements. Flower stems tend to be short and stubby. A beautiful variety but difficult to manage. Low spreading habit.

**Perfecta** (103)  HT

Raised by Kordes, Holstein, Germany

Introduced 1957

*Parentage* Golden Sceptre × Karl Herbst

More properly known as 'Kordes Perfecta', to distinguish it from a 1920 introduction no longer in commerce. Creamy yellow flushed pink. A true exhibition type rose with up to seventy petals tightly curled round a high centre. The early blooms seem to be prone to thrip damage and can look very untidy but the later blooms if carefully shielded can justify the implications of the variety's name. The tree are tall with long upright flower stems, albeit with weak necks that sometimes snap off in the wind. A variety best retained as a challenge to the amateur exhibitor who is acquainted with a few disappointments in his search for perfection. Medium to tall habit.

**Perle de Montserrat** (254)   M
Raised by Dot, Barcelona, Spain
Introduced 1945
*Parentage* Cecil Brunner × Rouletii
Pink edged with pearl. One of the really tiny miniatures that became popular upon their introduction just after the Second World War. Their tiny form was demonstrated by their being able to pass through a wedding ring. Many of the early varieties were plagued with mildew, although this variety still survives because of its healthy, if somewhat small, constitution. Often used as a cut rose in miniature flower arrangements. Plants usually grow to around 15 cm (6 in) high.

**Piccadilly** (75)   HT
Raised by McGredy, Auckland, New Zealand
Introduced 1960
*Parentage* McGredy's Yellow × Karl Herbst
Base gold flushed with deep orange with yellow reverse. Big blooms formed of as few as twenty-five broad petals are quick to open and show off their cheerfully bright colours. One of the first roses to bloom each season. Bushes can grow up to 1.2 m (4 ft) tall if lightly pruned. They are clothed in dark green glossy broad leaves which are not subject to any of the diseases of the rose, all

qualities that add up to make this the best of the bi-coloured hybrid teas.

**Picasso** (141)   F
Raised by McGredy, Auckland, New Zealand
Introduced 1971
*Parentage* Marlene × (Evelyn Fison × (Orange Sweetheart × Fruhlingsmorgen))
Silver and white with splashes of crimson and carmine. Silvery reverse. Each petal is slightly different, and this feature gave rise to the term 'hand painted roses'. The blooms are moderately full, twenty-five petals, borne several together and in trusses. Compact bushy habit to 75 cm (2½ ft) with small matt, medium green foliage. The first variety to be introduced with this type of distinctive colouring.

**Pink Favourite** (29)   HT
Raised by Von Abrams, California, USA
Introduced 1956
*Parentage* Juno × (Georg Arends × New Dawn)
Silvery rose pink. The bloom is long and pointed in the bud and the petals reflex strongly showing off the light pink of the upper face and the deeper rose pink on the underside of innermost petals which creates a shimmering effect. Some of the finest exhibition blooms ever shown have been produced by this rose which

responds to early disbudding and generous feeding. The foliage is especially noteworthy, very broad, very glossy and extremely disease-resistant. Healthy bushes in the medium to tall range.

**Pink Parfait** (161)  F
Raised by Swim, California, USA
Introduced 1960
*Parentage* First Love × Pinocchio
Satin pink flushed yellow. A variety beloved of flower arrangers for its constant production of petite tight buds that enable them to create dainty table arrangements. The flowers combine the biscuit shades at the base of the petal and deeply veined pink to gay effect. A tall sturdy bush with an upright habit and a generous free-flowering habit. Medium to tall grower.

**Pink Perpetue** (224)  C
Raised by Gregory, Nottingham, England
Introduced 1965
*Parentage* Spectacular × New Dawn
Bright rose pink. A repeat-flowering climber that flowers in clusters. Best described as an improved 'Zephirine Drouhin' as it has the same quantity of fragrant blooms but none of the mildew that regularly devastates the 'thornless rose'. To hurry on the next crop of blooms it is advisable to cut off the seed pods and oblige the plant to commence the reproduction cycle over again. Growth

is up to 3.6 m (12 ft) high. Suitable for house walls, pillars, pergolas or fences.

**Polly Perkins** (10)  HT
Raised by Gregory, Nottingham, England
Introduced 1967
*Parentage* Pink Favourite × unknown
Deep coral salmon. Diminutive, well-shaped blooms, several to the stem, are slow to develop and hold their bud-like form well into maturity. Bushes have a big spread but remain on the short side whilst providing lots of fragrant small sized buds ideal for decorative work. Short sturdy bushes clothed in broad, glossy green foliage.

**Pour Toi** (260)  M
Raised by Dot, Barcelona, Spain
Introduced 1946
*Parentage* Eduardo Toda × Pompon de Paris
Ivory white. Beautifully formed buds long and slender, perfectly proportioned for small flower arrangements. Unusually long stems for a miniature and very good weathering qualities for a white rose. Plants grow 15–20 cm (6–8 in) high and are suited to pots, troughs and rockeries.

**Precious Platinum** (108)  HT
Raised by Dickson, Co. Down, N. Ireland
Introduced 1974

*Parentage* Red Planet × Franklin Engleman

Rich bright crimson. High centred, symmetrical blooms of medium size, which have a strong fragrance and exceptionally good weathering qualities. All the blooms are held on top of luxuriantly foliaged plants, which are both disease-free and free-flowering. The blooms are a little on the small side for exhibition work but perfect for cutting or for bedding. This rose is the latest red rose from a hybridist who specialises in red hybrid teas and it carries all the qualities of a 'thoroughbred'. Plants are on the tall side and have an upright habit.

**Presumida** (285)      **M**

Raised by Dot, Barcelona, Spain

Introduced 1948

*Parentage* Edouardo Toda × Pompon de Paris

Apricot yellow. Crisp reflexing petals form a rather untidy flower, although it is double and long-lasting even in wet weather. The colour tends to fade in hot weather so that the outer petals bleach almost white. Distinguished because it was the first miniature with an apricot shade, and a welcome change from the reds, pinks and whites that were all that was available prior to its introduction. Plants grow 15–20 cm (6–8 in) high.

**Prima Ballerina** (79)      **HT**

Raised by Tantau, Holstein, Germany

Introduced 1957

*Parentage* unknown seedling × Peace

Strong rose pink blanching to silver. Long pointed blooms formed of large petals that first appear as a silvery pink and turn much deeper, especially at the edges as the bloom matures. The flowers are loosely petalled and are most suitable for making a show rather than for close examination. They are however extremely sweetly scented. The trees are very vigorous and can easily grow up to 1.2 m (4 ft) tall which suggests them as more suitable for a border than a formal rose bed. Its foliage and habit resemble that of the Peace rose, one of its parents.

**Princesse** (115)      **HT**

Raised by Laperriere, Rhone, France

Introduced 1964

*Parentage* (Peace × Magicienne) × (Independence × Radar)

Deep vermilion. A globular bud shape with the outer petals reflexing sharply to give them a spiky look. The petals are very crisp and firm and shrug off heavy rain without sustaining unsightly blemishes. The bushes are compact growers and do not seem inclined to reach much above 60 cm (2 ft) and all the flowers are borne on the top of the plants. The variety has two distinct flowering

171

periods which leaves an unfortunate gap with few flowers between the summer and autumn flushes. Medium upright habit.

**Queen Elizabeth** (129)  G
Raised by Lamments, California, USA
Introduced 1954
*Parentage* Charlotte Armstrong × Floradora
Clear orchid pink. Shapely high centred buds open into broad full blooms in large trusses. As soon as the centre bloom which will inevitably have the quality of a hybrid tea is over the flower truss bursts into a bouquet of bloom. The trees are so large and prolific that a new name, 'grandiflora', had to be coined to accommodate the type. The only problems experienced with this rose is that they tend to outgrow their welcome in a restricted site. A variety suitable for informal hedges and borders. Plants can grow unsupported to over 1.5 m (5 ft) high.

**Queen Elizabeth** (129)  C
A climbing sport of the bush grandiflora rose. The climbing form is even more vigorous than the bush and grows much too tall for most situations. Flowering is delayed as a consequence of the extraordinary amount of growth the climber will produce and it is quite usual to wait for two or three years for the tree to bear a bloom.

**Red Cascade** (281)  C
Raised by Moore, California, USA
Introduced 1976
*Parentage* (*Rosa wichuraiana* × Floradora) × Magic Dragon
Crimson red. 2.5 cm (1 in) deep red flowers cover a plant that can spread as far as 1.5 m (5 ft) across yet not grow more than about 25 cm (10 in) high. Its habit is to repeat flower on stems that will drape over a retaining wall, earth bank or even hanging basket. Its big problem in the UK is its susceptibility to mildew. Grown as an outdoor plant its foliage is often disfigured to such an extent that it is unacceptable as a commercial variety.

**Red Devil** (66)  HT
Raised by Dickson, Co. Down, N. Ireland
Introduced 1970
*Parentage* Silver Lining × Prima Ballerina
Scarlet with a light reverse. Large high pointed blooms with over seventy petals each. A rose that must have won more UK 'first prizes' than any other red hybrid tea in the UK. Consistent, quality blooms on healthy vigorous plants have endeared this variety to exhibitors who cherish and guard its extravagant blooms. It is not, however, a good garden rose owing to its poor weathering characteristics. Tall vigorous grower.

**Rise 'n' Shine** (284)  M
Raised by Moore, California, USA

Introduced 1977
*Parentage* Little Darling × Yellow Magic
Deep golden yellow. Generally accepted to be the best yellow miniature. Hybrid tea shaped buds retain their double form well into maturity and do not lose their colour as they develop into flowers that can reach up to 3.8 cm (1½ in) across. Plants have lots of upright flower stems and grow upwards of 25 cm (10 in). A very good cutting rose suitable for exhibition.

**Rob Roy** (184)                          F
Raised by Cocker, Aberdeen, Scotland
Introduced 1970
*Parentage* Evelyn Fison × Wendy Cussons
Deep crimson-scarlet. Blooms almost large enough to be classed as a hybrid tea are produced in neat clusters on long straight flower stems. A neat and tidy, clean-looking bush, completely free from disease. The clearest red floribunda and most attractive of its type yet introduced. Moderately tall upright habit.

**Rose Gaujard** (40)                     HT
Raised by Gaujard, Isere, France
Introduced 1957
*Parentage* Peace × Opera seedling
A confection of silvery white, pale pink and cherry pink. The petals appear to be almost striped with their bars of pink laid over the basically white petal. The blooms

are very high centred and since they have up to eighty petals each are often used for exhibition. A large quantity of seemingly immaculate blooms have the disquieting habit of revealing a split centre just when they should be reaching perfection. The vigorous and free-flowering plants also suit it for general garden use. However, its very distinctive appearance does not suit all tastes. Vigorous bushy grower with good, clean glossy foliage.

**Rosemary Rose** (186)                   F
Raised by de Ruiter, Hazerswoude, Holland
Introduced 1954
*Parentage* Gruss an Teplitz × unnamed seedling
Currant red suffused pink. Most unusual pompon-shaped flat blooms in heavy clusters. Also unusual for a floribunda type is its exceptional fragrance. The foliage imitates the dusky red colour of the flower and displays more bronze leaves than green. In season the bush is dressed top to toe in flower with trusses that tend if anything to be a bit top heavy with bloom and touch the ground when weighted. The bushes are inclined to suffer very badly from white powdery mildew. Medium height bushy habit.

**Rosina** (265)                          M
Raised by Dot, Barcelona, Spain
Introduced 1951

173

*Parentage* Eduardo Toda × Rouletii

Sunflower yellow. A shapely bloom in the bud stage has too few petals to sustain its hybrid tea like appearance for very long and opens into a semi-double flower with not much heart. It was, however, the leading yellow miniature for over twenty years after its introduction and its faults, which include a tendency to fade in maturity, were long overlooked because there were no new contenders to challenge its beauty. A vigorous plant growing up to 38 cm (15 in) tall.

**Rosy Cheeks** (100)          HT
Raised by Anderson, Aberdeen, Scotland
Introduced 1975
*Parentage* unknown × Grandpa Dickson
Flame red and gold. A real bi-colour red on the face of the petal yellow on the reverse. Petals are so large they can form a bloom of up to 20 cm (8 in) across. Not content with being a colourful flamboyant rose it exudes an attractive perfume. Blooms are held both on top and nestled inside the foliage of the plant. Its habit of growth is to produce strong sturdy bushes, not too tall or greedy for space, and its 'flower power' exceeds that of most varieties and makes it an ideal bedding rose.

**Rouletii** (286)          M
Discovered by Major Roulet in 1918
*Parentage* unknown
Rose pink. Generally held to be the forebear of all miniature roses. Its origins are unknown save that it was discovered by Major Roulet growing in pots on the window ledges of Swiss cottages. Since its dwarf habit remains genetically dominant it can be claimed that it is the founder of the modern race of miniature roses. A tidy little plant flowering in clusters and growing to around 25 cm (10 in).

**Royal Dane**          HT
See **Troika**

**Royal Gold** (227)          C
Raised by Morey, California, USA
Introduced 1957
*Parentage* Climbing Goldilocks × Lydia
Deep golden yellow. A shapely bloom with hybrid tea form and a fruity fragrance. Flowers in small clusters of three blooms with a recurrent habit. Plants only grow up to 2.4 m (8 ft) high and have a tendency to be on the 'soft' side so are liable to die back following a severe winter. This variety is considered to possess the most elegant flowers of any yellow climber.

**Royal Highness** (27)          HT
Raised by Swim & Weeks, California, USA
Introduced 1962
*Parentage* Virgo × Peace

Creamy pink. Blooms that have all the qualities of a good exhibition rose. High pointed centres that hold tight until the bloom is on the point of collapse and broad outer petals that give size and quality to a bloom that can be expected to grow 13–15 cm (5–6 in) across. A pleasant 'tea' fragrance that must be a characteristic inherited from its tea rose ancestors many generations back. Sad to say this variety is intolerant of rain and bruises easily. It is, however, a very good grower—strong, vigorous and disease-resistant. Medium height bushes.

**Royal Show** (90)                    HT
Raised by Gregory. Nottingham, England
Introduced 1973
*Parentage* Queen Elizabeth × unknown
Deep crimson. Big, broad, high centred exhibition style bloom. Petals are broad and 'fleshy' and impart a look of quality to the bloom. The blooms are so full and consequently slow to open that they do sustain a lot of weather damage, especially in the UK. Reports from Australia would have it one of their finest show roses ever. A robust, medium to tall bush, long stiff flower stems with strong necks.

**Ruby Wedding** (33)                  HT
Raised by Gregory, Nottingham, England
Introduced 1979

*Parentage* Mayflower × unknown
Deep ruby-red. The velvet-like inner surface of the petals contrasting with a lighter matt centre gives a pleasing effect. Blooms have an attractive sharp fragrance and hold their heads erect on stiff-necked stems. Bushes are vigorous, clothed in a dark green glossy and bronze foliage and grow to around the 75 cm (2½ ft) mark. Free from mildew, the blight of many a red rose.

**Rumba** (176)                        F
Raised by Poulsen, Kvistgaard, Denmark
Introduced 1958
*Parentage* Masquerade × (Poulsen's Bedder × Floradora)
Yellow and poppy-red. The ultimate development of the multi-coloured Masquerade theme. Full double blooms with as many as thirty-five petals each have bright yellow centres and a glowing red surround. Young buds are more inclined towards yellow; the mature blooms turn altogether crimson. A cheerful rose which does, however, require to be dead-headed regularly to remove spent bloom that tends to hold on to the stems for too long. A medium height bush clothed in light green glossy foliage.

**Sarabande** (154)                    F
Raised by Meilland, Cap d'Antibes, France
Introduced 1959

175

*Parentage* Cocorico × Moulin Rouge

Bright orange red. Semi-double blooms display their true beauty when fully open to form a dazzling show of colour. The extra prominent yellow stamens contrast with the clear orange of the petals in a bloom of around 6 cm (2½ in) across. Flowers are borne in broad clusters on low-growing bushes. Short bushy habit.

**Scarlet Gem** (248)  M

Raised by Meilland, Cap d'Antibes, France

Introduced 1961

*Parentage* (Moulin Rouge × Fashion) × (Perle de Montserrat × Perla de Alcanada)

Orange scarlet. Flowers made up of up to sixty slender pointed petals packed so tight that they can last over a week. Blooms keep their colour well and are produced regularly on compact bushes that grow to around 25 cm (10 in) high. The colour and compact form suggest it as suitable for a rockery.

**Schneewittchen**  F

See **Iceberg**

**Schoolgirl** (222)  C

Raised by McGredy, Auckland, New Zealand

Introduced 1964

*Parentage* Coral Dawn × Belle Blonde

Apricot-orange fading to salmon pink. Large, sweetly scented hybrid tea shaped flowers held individually or in small clusters of three blooms to the stem. A tree well clothed in glossy dark-green foliage and growing to around 3.6 m (12 ft) high. There is a tendency for the base of the climber to become bare if the basal shoots are not trained outwards, thus encouraging the laterals to shoot and provide both cover and flower.

**Serenade** (51)  HT

Raised by Boerner, New York State, USA

Introduced 1949

*Parentage* Sonata × R.M.S. Queen Mary

Coral-orange. A rather loose flower composed of broad flat petals. The beauty of the bloom lies in its clear pastel shade which at the time of its introduction was a refreshing new tone for hybrid teas. By modern standards neither the bloom nor the colour would be particularly outstanding, though its ability to open in wet weather would always be welcome. Tall upright grower.

**Shakespeare Festival** (249)  M

Raised by Moore, California, USA

Introduced 1979

*Parentage* Golden Angel × Golden Angel

Clear golden yellow. Loosely-formed buds of very strong unfading yellow, which on strong growing bushes tend to make for a decorative plant rather than an immaculate cutting variety. The blooms have a tea fragrance and are very freely produced on 25–38 cm (10–15 in) high plants.

**Sheri Anne** (237)    M
Raised by Moore, California, USA
Introduced 1973
*Parentage* Little Darling × New Penny
Orange red with a yellow base. A glowing, colourful bud opens out into a long lasting semi-double bloom. Plants grow well almost anywhere and suit this variety for pots, troughs, rockery or borders. An excellent variety for producing cut blooms for corsage, table decorations and exhibition. Bushes grow around 30 cm (1 ft) tall when established.

**Silver Jubilee** (76)    HT
Raised by Cocker, Aberdeen, Scotland
Introduced 1978
*Parentage* (Highlight × Colour Wonder) × (Parkdirektor Riggers × Piccadilly) × Mischief
A confection of coppery-pink apricot and peach. The base of each perfectly formed bloom is shaded apricot which blushes into a coppery pink towards the edges of the petal. The underside of the petal provides a contrast of peach pink. The satin-textured blooms are delicately scented and supported by luxuriantly glossy foliage. The most disease-resistant variety grown. Winner of the Royal National Rose Society's premier award—the President's

International Trophy 1978. Medium upright habit.

**Silver Wedding** (63)    HT
Raised by Gregory, Nottingham, England
Introduced 1976
*Parentage* Blue Moon × Super Star
Creamy-white outer petals edge a honey-shaded centre that sometimes tints of gentle blush pink, depending upon the amount of sunshine the bloom experiences. Flowers are held several to the stem (unless deliberately disbudded) on bushes that grow to around 75 cm (2½ ft) high. Dark contrasting foliage sets off the white flowers.

**Simple Simon** (277)    M
Raised by Robinson, Nottingham, England
Introduced 1955
*Parentage* (*Rosa multiflora nana* × Mrs Pierre S. du Pont) × Tom Thumb
Rose pink with pearl edges. A rose that reveals its true beauty only when fully open. Pompon-shaped blooms around 3.8 cm (1½ in) across are fringed with a lighter pink. They last a long while both on the bush and as cut blooms. Stems are rather slender and are inclined to droop under the weight of the bloom. Dainty 25 cm (10 in) high plants.

**Sir Lancelot** (185)      F
Raised by Harkness, Hertfordshire, England
Introduced 1967
*Parentage* Vera Dalton × Woburn Abbey
Apricot yellow. Neat semi-double blooms are borne several together on slightly top-heavy clusters. Their bud form is particularly beautiful but there is a tendency for the colour to fade as the flower ages. The weight of flower and the size of the clusters tends to make the bush look a little untidy but there is no other floribunda with such an appealing apricot shade to compare with this variety in its first flush of bloom. A bushy medium habit plant with light green foliage that is suspect in 'black spot' country.

**Souvenir de Jacques Verschuren** (25)      HT
Raised by Verschuren, Haps, Holland
Introduced 1950
*Parentage* Katherine Pechtold × Orange Delight
Gold shaded orange and salmon. Long slender buds hold their elegant shape and are considered the ideal button-hole rose. Bushes have an unusually dark bronze foliage and a stiff upright habit. By modern standards the rose appears rather insignificant but in its day it was considered one of the most beautiful hybrid teas which heralded the shapely new pastel-shaded introductions that were

more tolerant in wet weather than the previously fancied big 'cabbage' roses.

**Spanish Orange** (150)      F
Raised by de Ruiter, Hazerswoude, Holland
Introduced 1966
*Parentage* unknown
Tangerine orange. Dainty camellia-shaped blooms are held in clusters on rather long 'leggy' sprays. A bright, cheerful colour, but the blooms all seem to be a little top-heavy and droop down to give a somewhat wilted appearance. A good grower but a bit untidy for the formal rose border. Tall upright habit.

**Spectacular**      C
See **Danse du Feu**

**Spek's Yellow** (62)      HT
Raised by Verschuren-Pechtold, Hazerswoude, Holland
Introduced 1950
*Parentage* Golden Rapture × unnamed seedling
Also known as Golden Sceptre. Chrome yellow. Small but shapely blooms of button-hole proportions held several to the stem rather like a floribunda. Although the necks are a little wiry the colour lasts well without fading. At the time of its introduction most yellows had paler and fuller blooms which were inclined to fade and go rotten on the stem. A rather 'leggy' and by modern standards unruly grower, but a variety that is re-

178

membered for its consistent good nature in spite of inclement UK summers. Tall, untidy grower.

**Stacey Sue** (242)  M
Raised by Moore, California, USA
Introduced 1976
*Parentage* Ellen Poulsen × Fairy Princess
Soft pearl pink with a deeper pink heart. One of the smallest miniatures to be introduced in recent years. Blooms remain under 2.5 cm (1 in) across when fully opened. Plants are very bushy and round, covered in glossy green foliage and flower from spring to frost.

**Stanley Gibbons** (69)  HT
Raised by Gregory. Nottingham, England
Introduced 1976
*Parentage* Fragrant Cloud × Papa Meilland
Brick red with salmon orange reverse. Perfectly-shaped hybrid tea blooms in miniature. Strictly speaking, this is a floribunda hybrid tea type which was selected by the sponsors to be of special interest to flower arrangers. It can be relied upon to produce enough blooms for a small arrangement from a single flower truss, and every bud to be just the right size and form for a table decoration. Bushes are very free-flowering, healthy with dark glossy foliage and of medium habit.

**Starina** (253)  M
Raised by Meilland, Cap d'Antibes, France
Introduced 1965
*Parentage* (Dany Robin × Fire King) × Perle de Montserrat
Vivid orange scarlet with a yellow base to the petal. Perfectly formed small hybrid tea shaped buds. Acknowledged to be one of the best exhibition miniatures, as well as producing some of the finest cut bloom for miniature flower arrangements. Plants grow well 25–30 cm (10–12 in) high.

**Stars 'n' Stripes** (247)  M
Raised by Moore, California, USA
Introduced 1977
*Parentage* unknown
Strawberry red and white. Every tiny bud and flower is striped with red and white. This may be too bold a concept for some gardeners but it cannot be denied that the bushes are very striking. A fairly tall-growing miniature, up to about 38 cm (15 in), well clothed in medium green foliage with the flowers spaced regularly over the bush. Very good for rockeries and borders where it can be planted to best effect in groups all of the same variety.

**Stella** (80)  HT
Raised by Tantau, Holstein, Germany
Introduced 1958
*Parentage* Horstmann's Jubilaumsrose × Peace
Ivory flushed carmine. Blooms are

composed of around forty broad petals heavily veined carmine on an ivory base. The outer petals are deep pink while the flower is still showing a creamy white centre, giving a bi-colour appearance that is not universally popular. A very good exhibition rose with a good 'quality' look. Bushes have a lot of 'Peace' in them, and they are tall, bushy and healthy.

**Stephanie Diane** (7)  HT
Raised by Bees, Chester, England
Introduced 1971
*Parentage* Fragrant Cloud × Cassandra
Scarlet red. A giant of an exhibition rose. Big ovoid blooms that hold their centres well, and are fragrant and reasonably weather-resistant. Blooms can be as large as 13 cm (5 in) across and very full; nevertheless it is a good garden rose. A big free-blooming plant with dark bronze glossy foliage. Important to note is its freedom from mildew and its good stiff neck. Many red roses lack these qualities. Tall, vigorous upright habit.

**Sterling Silver** (68)  HT
Raised by Fisher, Massachusetts, USA
Introduced 1957
*Parentage* unnamed seedling × Peace
Lilac to pale lavender. This was the first of the post war hybrid teas that might reasonably be called 'the blue rose'. Although it

was far from blue it had charm and delicacy that won it favour in the cut flower trade. The buds are urn-shaped and the petals are slightly crinkled at the edges in the young bloom. The flowers are extremely fragrant. As a garden rose its performance is disappointing, it is a shy grower and does not make a big enough bush. It is inclined to take a long time to get established and is somewhat prone to mildew. Medium sparse bushes.

**Strawberry Fair** (189)  F
Raised by Gregory, Nottingham, England
Introduced 1966
*Parentage* Orangeade × unknown
Strawberry red. A pretty floribunda with neat double blooms in broad flat clusters. A bright colour though not altogether as popular as a crimson or scarlet rose of its short compact habit might have expected to be. Bushes are smothered in bloom and a continuous hedge-like effect can be achieved by planting at 45 cm ($1\frac{1}{2}$ ft) intervals. Bushes are tidy, compact, healthy growers, to around about 45 cm ($1\frac{1}{2}$ ft) tall.

**Strawberry Swirl** (238)  M
Raised by Moore, California, USA
Introduced 1978
*Parentage* Little Darling × unnamed seedling
An unusual blend of red, pink and white. The petals are splashed with broad stripes of colour but no two flowers are alike. Plants are

vigorous and healthy and grow slightly taller than most miniature bushes. A 40 cm (16 in) high plant covered with these extraordinary blooms is a splendid sight.

**Summer Holiday** (78)      HT
Raised by Gregory, Nottingham, England
Introduced 1967
*Parentage* Super Star × unknown
Vivid orange red. Blooms are composed of petals that curl back as soon as they begin to show colour to form a really furled high centred bloom. Although the flowers are quite large, especially when disbudded, a lot of split centres are revealed as the bloom develops. However, it is unrivalled in its colour category as a bedding rose. The bushes are sturdy and tall and bear flower at all heights and most generously throughout a long summer season. A tall and bushy habit equipped with a lot of thorns. A suitable variety for an informal rose hedge.

**Sunblest** (12)      HT
Raised by Tantau, Holstein, Germany
Introduced 1970
*Parentage* unnamed seedling × King's Ransom
Also known as Landora. Deep golden yellow. Long tubular-shaped buds composed of some forty-five widely spaced, broad flat petals that do not show much inclination to reflex even when the bloom is fully developed. This

effect can produce blooms that are often as large as 13 cm (5 in) across. A winning point with this rose is its ability to retain most of its deep colouring well into maturity. A bush that produces lots of branches dressed in glossy green foliage to back up the bright unfading blooms. Medium upright habit.

**Sunsilk** (38)      HT
Raised by Fryer, Cheshire, England
Introduced 1974
*Parentage* Pink Parfait × Redgold seedling
Bright lemon yellow. Flowers so freely it might well be in the floribunda category, were not the blooms so full of quality that one is obliged to acknowledge it as a hybrid tea. A perfect bedding rose producing masses of flower in big fragrant clusters, undoubtedly the best variety in its colour range. The blooms 'shatter' when fully developed and do not overstay their welcome as damaged decaying petals. This is a most important consideration with roses that produce blooms in big clusters. Very free-growing and flowering plants, in the medium to tall range.

**Super Star** (83)      HT
Raised by Tantau, Holstein, Germany
Introduced 1960
*Parentage* (seedling × Peace) × (seedling × Alpine Glow)
Also known as Tropicana. Pure

vermilion, the most attention-demanding colour ever seen in a rose. A refined, high centre bud formed of iridescent, clear fresh petals with a sharp apple-like fragrance. Several blooms to the stem can incline the bush to be slightly top-heavy but occasional dead-heading will overcome this slight drawback. The winner of the royal National Rose Society's Premier Award and all the Continental Rose Honours, also used extensively in breeding for new varieties. Growth is akin to that of a grandiflora, several blooms to the stem, tall and upright with an inclination to bloom at the top of the bush. Inclined to mildew in a bad season.

**Sutter's Gold** (65)                    HT
Raised by Swim, California, USA
Introduced 1950
*Parentage* Charlotte Armstrong × Signora
Orange opening to golden orange. Weather-resistant, long, tubular flowers that start as orange buds and then develop into golden flowers flushed with orange and pink. The blooms have an extraordinarily good fragrance and some of the longest straightest stems to be found on a hybrid tea. As a consequence of the latter the bushes are tall and upright growers and have dark, bronze foliage. A slightly disappointing feature of the blooms is that they open beyond their beautiful bud shape rather too quickly, but this

does account for their remarkable tolerance of wet weather conditions.

**Swan Lake** (214)                    C
Raised by McGredy, Auckland, New Zealand
Introduced 1968
*Parentage* Memorial × Heidelberg
White with a very soft pink centre. The ideal pillar rose, growing to around 3 m (10 ft) high. It is covered with clusters of fresh, almost weather-proof, white flowers. A repeat-flowering habit ensures there is always a show of bloom from spring to autumn. Arrange for the plant to have good support as the weight of bloom can cause the branches to hang low.

**Swedish Doll** (255)                    M
Raised by Moore, California, USA
Introduced 1976
*Parentage* Fire King × Little Buckeroo
Slender medium red buds open into lighter pinky-red flowers which, in full sunshine, age to a deeper red shade. Semi-double blooms up to 3.8 cm ($1\frac{1}{2}$ in) across when open are suitable for cutting and exhibition. Many-branched, rather upright plants are amongst the tallest of the miniatures and might be expected to grow over 38 cm (15 in) high.

**Sweet Fairy** (270)                    M
Raised by de Vink, Boskoop, Holland
Introduced 1946

*Parentage* Tom Thumb × unnamed seedling

Shell pink. It is surprising that a flower which develops to be no larger than 2.5 cm (1 in) across can hold so many petals. A dainty rose for the use in the smallest of miniature arrangements. Plants grow 15–20 cm (6–8 in) tall.

**Sympathie** (220)                    C

Raised by Kordes, Holstein, Germany

Introduced 1964

*Parentage* unknown

Dark red. Well-formed buds develop into rather loosely shaped flowers, each very sweetly scented. The colour tends to fade and turn slightly blue as the flowers develop. Plants are beautifully foliaged in dark green glossy foliage and grow to around 3.6 m (12 ft) high.

**Teneriffe** (109)                    HT

Raised by Bracegirdle, Nottingham, England

Introduced 1972

*Parentage* Fragrant Cloud × Piccadilly

Peach, yellow and orange. Pearshaped buds with tight centres can sometimes reach exhibition dimensions. The petals curl back very tightly as they open giving each a pointed appearance and a characteristic 'brittle' look to the bloom. The inside of the petals are a peachy yellow whilst their outer face is orange which the strong reflex serves to display to best

effect. The blooms are so fragrant that the variety has been awarded the Edland Memorial Trophy. A medium height bedding rose with most of the blooms held at the top of healthy plants.

**The Doctor** (52)                    HT

Raised by Howard, California, USA

introduced 1936

*Parentage* Mrs J.D. Eisele × Los Angeles

Satin pink. Double blooms that can be as large as 15 cm (6 in) across, if disbudded, produced in great profusion. If left to its own devices the plant will grow shrub like and cover itself with sweetly scented bloom. It is a variety that does not care to be pruned; a light trim is all that is necessary. Therefore a site that allows it to grow into a big bush is preferable. This American variety was brought into the UK just before the Second World War, so its impact on the rose market was somewhat diluted, and its beauty and generosity seem never to have been fully appreciated. Tall, bushy habit, an excellent informal hedging rose.

**The Queen** (56)                    HT

Raised by Lowe, Nottingham, England

Introduced 1954

*Parentage* Mojave × unknown

Orange flushed coral. A pointed bud opening to an urn-shaped bloom whose petals are embell-

183

ished with a neat frill that borders their outer edges. A sweetly scented cutting rose, lightly petalled, with long straight stems for cutting. A rose with good opening qualities but whose muted shades have no great visual impact. A medium height upright grower.

**Tip Top** (196)                    F
Raised by Tantau, Holstein, Germany
Introduced 1963
*Parentage* unknown
Also known as Baby Doll. Geranium pink with salmon shadings. Double blooms, full of petals, are more remarkable for their sheer quantity than their pleasing form. This is a low-growing variety that covers itself with short sprays of bloom so as to resemble a fragrant, compact cushion of roses. A variety that can be used in windy spots where taller growing varieties would take a battering. Neat and tidy growing habit up to around 45 cm (18 in).

**Tonnerre** (145)                   F
Raised by Mallerin, Isere, France
Introduced 1953
*Parentage* Holstein × Français
Dark crimson. Big blooms for a floribunda, composed of up to twenty-four velvet-like darkest crimson petals slowly opening to reveal bright golden stamens. Clusters of dusky red bloom are unusually large and dressed all over a bush furnished in dark green foliage. The plants are vigor-

ous and bushy but somewhat prone to mildew, which can completely spoil the dramatic impact of the plant.

**Topsi** (157)                      F
Raised by Tantau, Holstein, Germany
Introduced 1971
*Parentage* Fragrant Cloud × Signalfeuer
Brilliant orange red. Masses of long-lasting semi-double blooms cover the bush so that it resembles a rounded velvet cushion of glowing red. A bushy branching plant that remains round and compact and shows little inclination to grow over 45 cm (18 in) tall. At least one nursery has recorded that this rose has sold twice as well as their most popular hybrid tea which gives a good idea of its versatility. It can be grown under taller bushes to hide their legginess, against low retaining walls without overwhelming the feature, as a tidy edge to paths and patios and in windy spots. Its one fault is that it is prone to black spot attack and a careful watch must be kept so that the symptoms can be treated as early as possible.

**Toy Clown** (263)                  M
Raised by Moore, California, USA
Introduced 1966
*Parentage* Little Darling × Magic Wand
White base with pink or red edge to the petals. A strikingly different little flower that can be used as

a cut flower or for exhibition work. A clean crisp bloom that avoids weather damage is produced on very long individual flower stems. Plants grow with a bushy habit at around 25 cm (10 in) high.

**Troika** (17)                                HT
Raised by Poulsen, Kvistgaard, Denmark
Introduced 1971
*Parentage* unknown
Also known as Royal Dane. Orange bronze and gold. Broad blooms sometimes 15 cm (6 in) across formed of multicoloured petals, broad on the outward edge of the bloom but smaller in the centre so as to give a shapely, wide appearance. Multicoloured roses as a rule are not noted for their fragrance. This one, however, is distinguished by its extraordinary perfume. A bushy upright plant furnished in dark glossy green foliage that wards off mildew and black spot. A tall to medium habit.

**Tropicana**                                HT
See **Super Star**

**Typhoon** (88)                                HT
Raised by Kordes, Holstein, Germany
Introduced 1972
*Parentage* Dr A.J. Verhage × Colour Wonder
Salmon pink and coppery orange shadings. Blooms are inclined to be on the small side for a hybrid tea but this is compensated for by

the plant's habit of producing three or four blooms to the stem. The blooms are very fragrant and their massed effect indicates a good bedding variety, always in bloom. Dark, crisp bronze foliage, healthy and disease-free.

**Tzigane** (55)                                HT
Raised by Meilland, Cap d'Antibes, France
Introduced 1951
*Parentage* Peace × J.B. Meilland
Red and yellow. A real bicolour, globular-shaped blooms composed of cup-shaped petals with an undiluted rose red colour on one side and a real yellow on the reverse. A colourful fragrant bedding rose that throws long straight stems with dark bronze foliage. Suspect in a bad mildew season.

**Vanda Beauty** (123)                                HT
Raised by Gregory, Nottingham, England
Introduced 1971
*Parentage* Gertrude Gregory × unnamed seedling
Deep golden yellow. Petite fragrant blooms that do not fade when open. Short rather brittle flower stems grow upright from the base of the plant to no higher than 45 cm (18 in). As a consequence of its short habit it is among the first roses to bloom each season, and can be as much as two weeks ahead of the main crop. Deep green glossy foliage, free from disease, furnishes a short but vigorous plant that ideally should

be planted at around 30 cm (1 ft) intervals.

**Vienna Charm** (110)　　　HT
Raised by Kordes, Holstein, Germany
Introduced 1963
*Parentage* Chantre × Golden Sun
Also known as Wiener Charme. Coppery orange. A very long elegant bud shape that can grow as large as 15 cm (6 in) across without being fully opened. Considering the size of the flower one might reasonably expect to count more than twice the amount of petals that compose the bloom since there are a mere twenty-seven or so, which is rather too few for an exhibition rose. Plants are a little on the tall side with long stems that expose the blooms to weather damage. Tall upright plants.

**Vilia** (149)　　　F
Raised by Robinson, Leicester, England
Introduced 1960
*Parentage* unknown
Coral pink. Pretty single blooms with prominently displayed golden stamens in large flat clusters. This lovely rose, introduced at a time when all the new floribundas were double, recaptured all the charm and delicacy of the old fashioned 'polyantha', but claims the vigour and freedom of flower of its contemporaries. It has an unusually sweet fragrance. The bushes are medium height growers, holding all the bloom

above their heads while clothed in deep green glossy foliage.

**Ville de Chine**　　　S
See **Chinatown**

**Violet Carson** (132)　　　F
Raised by McGredy, Auckland, New Zealand
Introduced 1964
*Parentage* Mme Leon Cuny × Spartan
Soft peach with a biscuit-coloured reverse. Particularly large blooms have the hybrid tea like formation desired by the floral artist. The buds last well as cut flowers and seem just the right size to impart a long-lasting fresh look to an arrangement. The colours are a bit insipid when planted *en masse*, added to which the old blooms are inclined to bleach. A good strong bush with dark glossy foliage.

**Virgo** (54)　　　HT
Raised by Mallerin, Isere, France
Introduced 1947
*Parentage* Blanche Mallerin × Neige Parfum
White with undertones of blush pink. Lightly petalled urn-shaped flowers make it a popular cut flower variety. Its relatively few petals ensures that it will open in wet weather even if it does sustain a lot of unsightly brown blemishes. For over two decades after its introduction it remained unchallenged as the premier white hybrid tea. By modern standards it is rather shy and has low mildew

resistance. Medium height rather thin bushes that manage to produce long individual flower stems.

**Vivacious** (146)          F
Raised by Gregory, Nottingham, England
Introduced 1971
*Parentage* Super Star × unknown
Phlox pink. Large pointed blooms open to look like a rosette-shaped bloom. Some thirty-five narrow petals arranged at regular intervals contribute towards an unusual formation that suggests the bloom is never fully open. the colour alas is rather too sombre to make a show and its very dark bronzed foliage contributes to its lacklustre appearance; otherwise it is a medium height, healthy, free-flowering variety.

**Wendy Cussons** (2)       HT
Raised by Gregory, Nottingham, England
Introduced 1960
*Parentage* Independence × Eden Rose
Rose red. Often described as the 'perfect English rose'. Very high centred, elegant blooms with damask perfume that show a distinct preference for cool weather. Grown at its most beautiful in the northern counties of England. A worthwhile exhibition rose as well as a reliable bedding rose. Bushes are branching and on the tall side, disease-free leathery dark green foliage. Perhaps its best recommendation is a list of some of its awards: RNRS President's Trophy, First Certificate Rome Trials, Award of Merit RHS, Golden Rose of the Hague.

**Westminster** (121)       HT
Raised by Robinson, Leicester, England
Introduced 1960
*Parentage* Gay Crusader × Peace
Cherry red and yellow. The blooms are best described as very highly coloured 'Peace' flowers. The young buds open with a bright red predominant and unfurl to show more of the gold flushed coppery salmon reverse petals. The blooms are extremely fragrant and won for the variety the Clay Challenge Trophy. Much of the 'Peace' vigour has been inherited by the bushes which are tall, healthy and well furnished.

**Whisky Gill** (101)       HT
Raised by Cobley, Leicester, England
Introduced 1972
*Parentage* a sport of Whisky Mac
Copper bronze. A deeper coloured version of the variety Whisky Mac of which it is a sport. Blooms have the characteristic frill of its parent, and also its fragrance. The foliage is perhaps a shade darker than the original. It is reasonably disease-free, although tender new secondary shoots are liable to mildew attack. Medium bushy habit.

**Whisky Mac** (71) HT
Raised by Tantau, Holstein, Germany
Introduced 1967
*Parentage* unknown
Deep harvest gold deepening towards tangerine on the inside of the petals. Classic shaped blooms at all stages of development. The petals have the suggestion of a frill to the edges of the petals adding to the interest of the flowers which are very sweetly scented. The bushes are exceptionally healthy for an apricot shaded rose which more often than not are subject to mildew attack. The new growth is an unusual red with thin elongated leaflets which give the erroneous impression that they are diseased. A medium bushy grower.

**White Knight** HT
See **Message**

**Wiener Charme** HT
See **Vienna Charm**

**Woman and Home** (53) HT
Raised by Gregory, Nottingham, England
Introduced 1976
*Parentage* Apricot Silk × Piccadilly seedling
Deep apricot yellow. Buds are composed of around thirty broad strongly reflexing petals. Though they look like an exhibition rose the centre breaks rather too quickly and is more suited to be a cutting rose. It is difficult to imagine a cut rose with more appeal than this high centred urn-shaped rose. Plants are on the tall side, very vigorous with a repeat-flowering habit.

**Woman's Realm** (73) HT
Raised by Gregory, Nottingham, England
Introduced 1966
*Parentage* Chrysler Imperial × unknown
Signal red. More accurately described as a floribunda hybrid tea type, as it has a strong inclination to produce clusters of bloom rather than individual specimens. The colour remains a bright glowing red as the petals fall just as they are about to turn blue with age. Vigorous upright habit to around 75 cm ($2\frac{1}{2}$ ft).

**Yellow Doll** (259) M
Raised by Moore, California, USA
Introduced 1962
*Parentage* Golden Glow × Zee
Creamy yellow. High centred fragrant blooms up to 3.8 cm ($1\frac{1}{2}$ in) across. Full double blooms of some fifty slender petals. The colour suits those who do not want to introduce too hard a yellow colour into their arrangements. Very free-flowering plants which grow to around 30 cm (1 ft) high.

**Yellow Petals** (107) HT
Raised by Robinson, Leicester, England
Introduced 1971

*Parentage* King's Ransom × Dorothy Peach

Golden yellow. Urn-shaped golden buds with a most unusual freesia-like fragrance. The blooms do pale off when fully open but always retain a delicate, pretty form. The bushes spread outwards rather than grow upright and present a problem as to where the gardener should stand when pruning the bushes. Short prostrate habit.

**Young Quinn** (117)                    HT

Raised by McGredy, Auckland, New Zealand

Introduced 1976

*Parentage* unknown

Deep golden yellow with a hint of pink at the tip of each outer petal. A big extravagant bloom that does not fade in strong sunshine and retains its deep yellow shades right up to the time of petal fall. Bushes are vigorous, upright growers around 75–100 cm (2½–3 ft) clothed in thick glossy foliage to protect them from disease.

**Zambra** (171)                    F

Raised by Meilland, Cap d'Antibes, France

Introduced 1961

*Parentage* (Goldilocks × Fashion) × (Goldilocks × Fashion)

Orange with a yellow reverse. An eye-catching combination of colours displayed by small clusters of semi-double blooms produced freely on medium height bushes. A novel shade rather spoilt by the susceptibility of the bush to mildew and black spot. Medium branching habit.

**Zephirine Drouhin** (223)                    C

Raised by Bizot, France

Introduced 1868

*Parentage* unknown

Rose pink. The 'thornless rose' possessed of remarkable fragrance and an abundance of bloom in its spring flush. The blooms are only semi-double and the reputation of the plant depends upon its ability to produce a mass of bloom rather than elegant flowers. The tree can grow up to 3.6 m (12 ft) high and have a good spread. The stems are devoid of thorns. The plant is very susceptible to mildew which can smother the plant in a disfiguring white powder.

# *Index*

Figures in **bold** refer to colour plates.

Alec's Red 122, **23**
Alexander 122, **58**
Allgold 122, **178**
Aloha 123, **213**
Altissimo 123, **226**
Ama 123, **169**
Amarillo 123, **74**
Andrea 123, **241**
Andre le Troquer 123, **36**
Anna Wheatcroft 124, **180**
Appreciation 124, **92**
Apricot Silk 124, **19**
Arthur Bell 124, 125, **163**
Autumn Sunlight 125, **219**

Baby Bio 125, **151**
Baby Darling 125, **269**
Baby Doll *see* Tip Top
Baby Gold Star 125, **274**
Baby Masquerade 125, **278**
Ballerina 126, **206**
Bambino 126, **267**
Beauté 126, **98**
Beauty Secret 126, **264**
Bengali 126, **191**
Bettina 127, **22**
Blessings 127, 59, **215**
Blue Moon 127, **5**
Bonn 127–8, **203**
Bonnie Scotland 128, **32**
Border Coral 128, **193**
Born Free 128, **276**
Buccaneer 128, **11**

Can Can 129, **61**
Casino 129, **217**
Centrex Gold 129, **153**
Champs Elysées 129, **82**
Charleston 129, **160**
Cherryade 130, **225**
Cheshire Life 130, **87**
Chicago Peace 130, **85**
Chinatown 130, **204**
Christian Dior 131, **15**
Cinderella 131, **287**

Circus 131, **142**
City of Belfast 131, **181**
City of Leeds 131, **165**
Cock o' the North 132, **120**
Compassion 132, **210**
Coralin 132, **282**
Coral Queen Elizabeth 132, **147**
Coral Silk 132, **172**
Corso 133, **111**
Cover Girl 133, **30**

Dale Farm 133, **131**
Danse du Feu 133, **212**
Darling Flame 133–4, **243**
Dearest 134, **136**
Deep Secret 134, **64**
Diorama 134, **8**
Doc 134, **156**
Doreen 135, **57**
Dorothy Wheatcroft 135, **200**
Double Joy 135, **250**
Dr A. J. Verhage 135, **43**
Dr Albert Schweitzer 135–6, **89**
Dresden Doll 136, **229**
Dr John Snow 136, **84**
Duftwolke *see* Fragrant Cloud
Duke of Windsor 136, **125**
Dutch Gold 136, **50**
Dwarf King 137, **273**

Easter Morning 137, **283**
Eleanor 137, **275**
Electron *see* Mullard Jubilee
Elizabeth Harkness 137, **116**
Elizabeth of Glamis 137–8, **187**
Ena Harkness 138, **34**
Ernest H. Morse 138, **114**
Etude 138, **216**
Europeana 138–9, **143**
Evelyn Fison 139, **174**

Fairy Magic 139, **230**
Fashion 139, **144**
Fashion Flame 139, **279**
Fire Princess 140, **256**
Fleur Cowles 140, **130**
Fragrant Cloud, 140, **46, 209**

Fred Loads 141, **207**
Frensham 141, **168**

Garden Party 141, **127**
Gay Gordons 141, **96**
Gay Maid 142, **133**
Glenfiddich 142, **177**
Gold Coin 142, **268**
Golden Angel 142, **235**
Golden Giant 142, **16**
Golden Sceptre *see* Spek's Yellow
Golden Showers 143, **211**
Golden Times 143, **3**
Golden Treasure 143, **138**
Goldgleam 143, **190**
Goldmarie 144, **183**
Goldschatz *see* Golden Treasure
Green Diamond 144, **239**
Gypsy Jewel 144, **252**

Hamburg Love 144–5, **139**
Handel 145, **221**
Happy Thought 145, **240**
Harlow 145, **118**
Harriny 145, **37**
Heart of England 146, **126**
Herzog von Windsor *see* Duke of Windsor
Hula Girl 146, **271**

Iceberg 146, **164, 208**
Iced Ginger 146, **188**
Ice White 147, **197**
Indian Chief 147, **112**
Invitation 147, **119**
Isabel de Ortiz 147, **6**

Jamboree 148, **162**
Janice Tellian 148, **262**
Jean Rook 148, **67**
John Waterer 148, **97**
Josephine Bruce 149, **39**
Joseph's Coat 149, **199**
Journey's End 149, **105**
Joyce Northfield 149, **49**
Judy Fischer 150, **272**
Julia's Rose 150, **70**
June Time 150, **266**
Just Joey 150, **113**

Kara 150–1, **228**
Karl Herbst 151, **47**
Kassel 151, **201**
Kilworth Gold 151, **1**
King Arthur 151, **166**
King's Ransom 151–2, **28**
Köln am Rhein 152, **205**
Korona 152, **194**

Lady Belper 152, **60**
Lady Grade 152–3, **95**
Lady of the Sky 153, **124**
Lady Sylvia 153, **21**
Lancastrian 153, **128**
Landora *see* Sunblest
Lavender Jewel 154, **231**
Lavender Lace 154, **234**
Lavender Lassie 154, **202**
Lavender Princess 154, **195**
Lemon Delight 154, **233**
Leslie G. Harris 154–5, **104**
Leslie Johns 155, **72**
Lilli Marlene 155, **192**
Lily de Gerlache 155, **45**
Little Flirt 155–6, **258**
Living Fire 156, **148**
Lord Louis 156, **94**
Lovers' Meeting 156, **9**
Love Token 156, **134**

Madame Henri Guillot 157, **24**
Magic Carousel 157, **245**
Mainzer Fastnacht *see* Blue Moon
Manx Queen 157, **155**
Ma Perkins 157–8, **170**
Margaret Merril 158, **182**
Maria 158, **198**
Marlena 158, **152**
Mary Marshall 158–9, **251**
Masquerade 159, **137, 218**
Matangi 159, **167**
Mayflower 159, **18**
McGredy's Sunset 160, **13**
McGredy's Yellow 160, **93**
Message 160, **99**
Mildred Scheel *see* Deep Secret
Mischief 160, **4**
Mister Lincoln 161, **42**
Mojave 161, **41**
Monique 161, **14**
Montezuma 161, **86**
Mood Music 162, **232**
Mrs Sam McGredy 162, **26**
Mullard Jubilee 162, **106**
My Choice 162–3, **35**
My Girl 163, **175**
My Valentine 163, **257**

New Penny 163, **261**
News 163, **140**
Nozomi 164, **280**

Orangeade 164, **135**
Orange Honey 164, **246**
Orange Sensation 164, **159**
Orange Silk 165, **173**
Over the Rainbow 165, **244**

**191**

Paddy McGredy 165, **179**
Pamela's Choice 165–6, **44**
Panorama Holiday 166, **91**
Papa Meilland 166, **31**
Paprika 166, **158**
Paris Match 167, **77**
Pascali 167, **122**
Peace 167, **81**
Peachy White 167–8, **236**
Pebble Mill 168, **20**
Percy Thrower 168, **48**
Perfecta 168, **103**
Perle de Montserrat 169, **254**
Piccadilly 169, **75**
Picasso 169, **141**
Pink Favourite 169, **29**
Pink Parfait 170, **161**
Pink Perpetue 170, **224**
Polly Perkins 170, **10**
Pour Toi 170, **260**
Precious Platinum 171, **285**
Prima Ballerina 171, **115**

Queen Elizabeth 172, **129**

Red Cascade 172, **281**
Red Devil 172, **66**
Rise 'n' Shine 172–3, **284**
Rob Roy 173, **184**
Rose Gaujard 173, **40**
Rosemary Rose 173, **186**
Rosina 174–4, **265**
Rosy Cheeks 174, **100**
Rouletii 174, **286**
Royal Dane *see* Troika
Royal Gold 174, **227**
Royal Highness 174, **27**
Royal Show 175, **90**
Ruby Wedding 175, **33**
Rumba 175, **176**

Sarabande 175–6, **154**
Scarlet Gem 176, **248**
Schneewitchen *see* Iceberg
Schoolgirl 176, **222**
Serenade 176, **51**
Shakespeare Festival 176, **249**
Sheri Anne 177, **237**
Silver Jubilee 177, **76**
Silver Wedding 177, **63**
Simple Simon 177, **277**
Sir Lancelot 178, **185**
Souvenir de Jacques Verschuren 178, **25**
Spanish Orange 178, **150**
Spectacular *see* Danse du Feu

Spek's Yellow 178, **62**
Stacey Sue 178, **242**
Stanley Gibbons 179, **69**
Starina 179, **253**
Stars 'n' Stripes 179, **247**
Stella 179–80, **80**
Stephanie Diane 180, **7**
Sterling Silver 180, **68**
Strawberry Fair 180, **189**
Strawberry Swirl 180, **238**
Summer Holiday 181, **78**
Sunblest 181, **12**
Sunsilk 181, **38**
Super Star 181–2, **83**
Sutter's Gold 182, **65**
Swan Lake 182, **214**
Swedish Doll 182, **255**
Sweet Fairy 182–3, **270**
Sympathie 183, **220**

Tenerife 183, **109**
The Doctor 183, **52**
The Queen 183–4, **56**
Tip Top 184, **196**
Tonnerre 184, **145**
Topsi 184, **157**
Toy Clown 184–5, **263**
Troika 185, **17**
Tropicana *see* Super Star
Typhoon 185, **88**
Tzigane 185, **55**

Vanda Beauty 185, **123**
Vienna Charm 186, **110**
Vilia 186, **149**
Ville de Chine *see* Chinatown
Violet Carson 186, **132**
Virgo 186, **54**
Vivacious 187, **146**

Wendy Cussons 187, **2**
Westminster 187, **121**
Whisky Gill 187, **101**
Whisky Mac 188, **71**
White Knight *see* Message
Wiener Charm *see* Vienna Charm
Woman and Home 188, **53**
Woman's Realm 188, **73**

Yellow Doll 188, **259**
Yellow Petals 188–9, **107**
Young Quinn 189, **117**

Zambra 189, **171**
Zephirine Drouhin 189, **223**